The Adventures of a Lifeguard and other Short Stories
by
Willard Renalda Bean

as told to Pamela Ramsay

© 2021 Renalda Bean

All rights reserved. No part of this publication may be reproduced, distributed, or transmitted in any form or by any means, including photocopying, recording, or other electronic or mechanical methods, without the prior written permission of the publisher, except in the case of brief quotations embodied in critical reviews and certain other noncommercial uses permitted by copyright law.

For permission requests, contact Mr. Willard Renalda Bean at 1-441-334-8835.

This book is a memoir. It reflects the author's present recollections of experiences over time. Some names and characteristics have been changed, some events have been compressed, and some dialogue has been recreated.

As told to Pamela Ramsay

Book design & editing by Natasha E. Bean

ISBN 978-0-947482-32-9

First printing edition, November 2021 in the United States

Published by lulu.com

Dedication

Dedicated to my Momma,
Marie Elouise Tuzo Bean Lodge.
I never got a chance to tell her these stories when she was alive,
and thinking about all my adventures through the years made me realize
what a special person she was bringing up ten children.
Her sacrifice and resilience lives within.

To my son,
Renalda Bermudaz Judiah Bean.
You loved life and made me proud in many ways. I was eager for you to know
these stories, to get a view of this beautiful island home you were named after.
I thank God for the life you lived and the impact you had on the world.

Table of Contents

Chapter	Title	Page
Chapter 1	My Formative Years With My Father	1
Chapter 2	The Brass Rail Restaurant	9
Chapter 3	Whatever Happened to my Spring Hill?	14
Chapter 4	Our First Television	18
Chapter 5	Male Predators	24
Chapter 6	The Manager's Wife and Her Poodle	26
Chapter 7	College Kids	29
Chapter 8	Blaming Blacks for Crimes They Did Not Commit	31
Chapter 9	The Peeping Tom Confession	36
Chapter 10	My Part-Time Night Job	39
Chapter 11	Desperate for a Babysitter	41
Chapter 12	Bermuda Hospitality	43
Chapter 13	Beautiful Translucent Bubbles	49
Chapter 14	When You Don't Listen, You Learn The Hard Way	51
Chapter 15	Now You Know What Pain Feels Like	53
Chapter 16	The Undercurrent	56
Chapter 17	Miss Jane	60

Chapter 18	Who Respects Who	62
Chapter 19	The Red-Haired Man and His New Position	65
Chapter 20	The Red-Haired Lady and Her New Volkswagen	69
Chapter 21	The Bermuda Triangle Mysteries	73
Chapter 22	Waterspouts and Tornadoes	77
Chapter 23	Shark Attack	80
Chapter 24	Mike and His Red Dinghy	84
Chapter 25	A Lifeguard's Duty- The Untold Story of a Heroic Rescue	87
Chapter 26	Celebrity Guests	92
Chapter 27	My Three Best Friends	94
Chapter 28	You Are Officially in The Race	98
Chapter 29	Going to the Record Hops	104
Chapter 30	It's All in Divine Order	107
Chapter 31	Second Act	114
-	Conclusion	117
-	Addendum	118
-	About the Author	121
-	About the Amanuensis	122
-	About the Editor	123

CHAPTER ONE
My Formative Years with My Father

I have very vivid memories of my father. My stories begin with the time spent with him up to the age of eight years old, when my father unfortunately met with his untimely death at the age of twenty-nine, while working for the United States Navy at the Naval Annex in Southampton, Bermuda. During his time working on the base my father did many jobs, such as working in the machine shop, driving buses, and driving the base trucks transporting goods from one base to another in St. Georges, Bermuda. He was definitely a "Jack of All Trades" and they appreciated him for his worth. While the U.S. military were stationed in Bermuda, the White Officials of the Bermuda Government told the U.S. Officials that they were not to pay the Black Bermudians the same rate as the White Bermudians. This was during the days of racial segregation which was prevalent all over at that time, but the U.S. Officials did not take their 'advice' and they paid the Black Bermudians the same wage as the White Bermudians who were under their employ.

The U.S. Base Officials always looked out for the Bermudian families in a good way, and one of the best things we Bermudians looked forward to was holidays- especially every Thanksgiving, Christmas, and 4th of July. At Thanksgiving, the U.S. Base Officials would come to the house to pick the whole family up and carry us to the base to celebrate with large amounts of food for all. Another holiday we always enjoyed was Christmas, when Bermudian children whose parents worked for the base would be invited to their annual Christmas Party, with food, fun and all the great toys that were given to the children.

In 1946, motor vehicles were introduced to Bermuda by an Act of Parliament. This Act allowed private cars and taxis to be operated independently. My father was still working for the U.S. base, but he also began to work part-time driving for the taxi company for additional income. To this day, after 75 years, I can still remember the make of the taxi, which was a Desoto. My first real memory with my father begins at the age of five, when he put me on a horse for the first time by myself. I was so frightened I screamed my head off, and he just calmly took me off. Before that, he used to ride with me on the horse and I was fine, but being by myself up there was scary to a child. He calmly kept putting me back on the horse gradually until finally, I was relaxed. He walked next to me as I was on the horse, and from that day on, I enjoyed riding horses up to the time of his death.

Another one of my fond memories of my father was that he was a "Father" to all of the neighborhood children, and he would teach them to spin tops, play "Backyard Cricket" and marbles. Marbles was a big game for all of the children, it was one of the biggest things for Bermudian children to play. Everyone had a backyard and both girls and boys all wanted to play marbles. The idea of the game was you win one another's marbles, which can leave you with a big collection if you were good. Most of them I won- everyone loved marbles.

On a Saturday afternoon about three-thirty p.m., four guys came to my house and knocked on my door. My mother opened the door and one of the guys said, *"Good afternoon Ms. Bean, is Big Load home?"* My mother smiled, because she knew that was my nickname, and she knew all their nicknames as well. She called me saying, *"Renalda, your friends are here."* Nicknames are very popular to many guys and girls. I came to the door to see who they were, King Load, Crow, Donkey and Golf Ball. *"Hey guys, what's up?"* Crow said, *"Poopy is having a big marble game over his house and he wants all of us to come."* We left my house, and as we started down Spring Hill, across the street we saw Spooky Bear, Cock Robin, Kilroy, Tack, and Bubble Head, and they joined us on the way. We passed six little girls, Sue, Pinky, Joey, Antee, Maggie and Twiddles sitting on Miss Guyah Wilsons steps. Further down the road, we met up with Outta Sight, Boots, and Cavity Guts. A little further along the road were two cousins, Pick Fowl and Funny Eyes who joined us. As we crossed Mr. Lee's Field, we came to the 'band- room', which was in the bushes. The band was made up of Sammy Dick, Forty, Jack Ugly, Plunger, Blacky, Big Mares, Leady and Jelly. This was a special place for these guys, as they sang and played all types of music, calypso, blues, Christmas tunes, gospel music and even some slave songs. The band-room was these guys' heaven. After passing the 'band-room' we were now at Poopy's house, where many of the other friends were waiting for us: Bop, May-Wing, Action, Bozo, Cat's Hair, Go Bell, Rat, and Poopy's uncle, Gobbles.

    My father was a skilled kite maker, and it is tradition in Bermuda to fly kites on Good Friday. Whenever he made kites, he would give one to all the neighborhood children. I think one of the best gifts he gave me was the knowledge and teachings on how to make kites, because in the years to come, this helped me support my mother by making beautiful kites and selling them to help the family.

Renalda & two of his sisters

Another memory of my father was the time that three of my neighbor's children told me that they could not get into their house, as the door was locked. The oldest boy proceeded to climb through the window, and when he came back out he said that his mother was asleep and he could not awaken her, so I went to call my father to tell him that the children could not awaken their mother. My father then went through their window, and once inside he discovered that their mother had died. Having realized these children's mother passed on, my father went to call her sisters and brothers who lived nearby, and sadly thereafter we lost our friends because they had to move in with relatives somewhere else.

One of the important lessons that I learned from my father was the time when he asked me to go to the grocery store, which he and my mother often did. He gave me the money, and I did not wait for him to tell me what he wanted, but I told him what he wanted; which were the same items every time I went to the store, bread, butter and ham. Once I repeated what I normally get for him, he didn't say anything and off I went. When I returned home, much to my surprise I got a whipping. After he whipped me, he told me that I must learn to listen before making my mind up of what he wanted, as he did not want ham this time, but he had wanted cheese. When I look back on my life, I realize that I have lived much of it following the examples and lessons I learned from my father.

    At the age of five, I used to walk home from school and cross the stone quarry and I would see the stonecutters doing their work. At that age I became very interested in quarry work. Stonecutters were needed in Bermuda because the buildings at that time were built of limestone. The cutters would cut limestone down and cut slate out of the limestone for the roofs. These stones can be very porous, therefore the stonecutters had to evaluate a stone to see how to get the best cut. The roofs are painted white as part of the purification of the rainwater, which is collected and flowed into tanks. Back then, all the Bermuda roofs were made out of limestone and wooden frames, and still they have not found anything to replace the limestone in roofs. So, I would dash home to take my suitcase and lunch kit, and go back to the quarry to watch the workers, knowing that I had to be back home before my father got home. When the stonecutters finished, I knew that I had to be on my way home fast.

    On this particular day, at the age of eight, I remember when I got home from the quarry I found my mother, siblings and neighbors at my house and they were all crying. There were two policemen there and before anyone could tell me anything, I immediately knew that something had happened to my father. You see, my father had many jobs, one of them was working with metal. It was told that my father got a piece of metal stuck in his hand and it had become infected. On his way home while riding the bus, my father died.

I instantly ran back to the quarry and just sat down on a rock until it was pitch dark. While sitting in the darkness, all I could think of was "*What am I going to do to help my mother?*" When I returned home, there were two of our neighbors who were Portuguese ladies there consoling my mother, and when they saw me, they both came to hug me and started to cry. I just pulled away from them and went to my room. The next morning, everything went on as normal, my mother fixing breakfast and I went off to school. When I returned home later that day, they told me that they had buried my father, which was the very same day my youngest sister turned one. Back in those days, because they did not have refrigerators, once you passed away, you were buried the next day. It left little time for mourning, but memories of my father will live with me forever.

After the death of my father, I became more interested in working at the quarry, so every day after school I went there and I started to do little odd jobs, like picking up broken stones and clearing them out of the way, as this is something that I had observed the stone cutters do on a number of occasions. One day, one of the owners, a Mr. Simons observed my eagerness to work in the quarry, and handed me a small saw and from that day on I became one of the best stonecutters. I knew the whole trade at the tender age of thirteen and could channel the block down, cut it up in pieces, and determine the best cuts. You needed to have strength, skill and determination to do the lifting and rolling of the stones as this was all physical work. It was one of the most physical jobs I have ever had, and you had to know if your block broke in half or three pieces, you had to know how to get the most out of the pieces. Mr. Simons was impressed, and gave me his portion of the quarry along with his tools to work, as he wanted to retire soon. At the time when Mr. Simon's handed over his portion of the quarry to me, it was well known that I was the youngest stonecutter to own his own portion of a quarry, and the older stonecutters in the other quarries around the island were so impressed that they use to come by the quarry just to see me work!

Two months after receiving ownership of my portion of the quarry, I found all my blocks had been taken. This happened quite a few times and it became a nuisance. Generally, if someone took something they would come back and pay you, so I assumed for the first couple of times someone would come and pay me for the stones I had worked. After a few times of this happening, a woman who lived nearby told me that she had seen a man who she knew come to the quarry in a truck at night when no one was there and take my blocks. When she told me the name of the man, I knew him because I was going to school with his children. Of course, when I approached him, he denied it, but the lady identified him. He still did not pay me for the several hundred stolen blocks, and I never saw him in that area again. The most disappointing thing to me about this incident was that the man knew my father had passed away and that I was helping my mother to support the family, and yet he would still do this to me.

When this incident happened, I went to Mr. Simons to explain to him that a trunk driver had been coming to the quarry and had stolen all of my blocks and I never got paid for all the work that I had done. I also told him that I had to give it up, as I needed to make some money to help my mother. When Mr. Simons heard this news, he was so upset that he actually cried. When I arrived home that evening and told my mother of what had been happening at the quarry, she shortly thereafter found a job for me at the Elbow Beach Hotel as an apprentice in the Carpenter Shop. I loved the quarry work, but did not want to do work and not be paid for it. I knew my worth, but ended up earning less at the Carpentry Shop, however I learned many more valuable lessons.

CHAPTER TWO
The Brass Rail Restaurant

Shortly after the death of my father my family of eleven, which included my mother, Marie, my sister Violeta (the oldest), my brother Larry (the second oldest) myself (the third oldest), my brother Melvin (the fourth oldest), the twins, Geraldine and Gerald (fifth and sixth), my sister Gilda (the seventh child), my brother Leon (the eighth child), my sister Verlice (the ninth child), and the youngest girl named Karen (the tenth and last); we had to move from our house on Billy Goat Hill in Warwick to my Granny Tuzo's house who lived on Court Street in the City of Hamilton. While we were staying with my Granny Tuzo, my mother was looking very hard for a place where she could have her whole family together, because she did not want to see her family split up.

We were at Granny Tuzo's home for about four to six months, and one Saturday afternoon, my mother took me to see a house located on Spring Hill, Warwick, which I fell in love with as soon as I walked in, as it felt like being in heaven. Later, I found out that the house was actually called "The Poor House," but it felt like a king's castle to me. My mother then said to me with much excitement, "*In two days everyone is going to be home together.*" When we moved into the "Poor House," the seven oldest children were in school, and the three youngest were at home with our mother. The house consisted of two bedrooms, a kitchen, and there was an outhouse out back. One bedroom which was larger was shared by my five sisters and my mother, and the other bedroom was shared by the five boys

At this time our mother was receiving help from the U.S. Navy, where my father had worked up until his death, and while at home taking care of the three youngest children, to help out with our expenses, our mother had women come to the house and she would hot press their hair. My mother also sewed dresses for women and family members, and also made all of our clothing, including our underwear which she made from flour bags.

Years later, when we were all at an age to attend school, my mother started to get jobs outside of the home, and this began with my mother going to some of our White neighbors and asking them if they needed her to do their washing, cooking, or house cleaning. When she got her first job, she would wait for all of us to come home from school, feed us, and she would then take me along to go to work for the "White Folks". At their homes, she would have to do house cleaning, washing, and cook their meals. After working with the first family for about three months, they were so impressed with her that they started telling their friends about her work and her cooking, that before you knew it, she became well known for her soups and ended up cooking soups for many White families in the neighborhood on Harbor side around snake road, Keith Hall Road.

Having worked for the neighborhood families for a while, the husband of one of the families Momma worked for, worked for one of the top restaurants on Queens Street in Hamilton called "The Brass Rail". He recommended my mother to the owner of the restaurant, commenting on her great soups, and she was hired to cook there. Once she started to work at The Brass Rail restaurant, my mother had started to teach her older daughters, Violeta, Geraldine and Gilda how to cook, so that they became responsible for cooking for the family. This allowed her to leave home every day at five-thirty p.m. to go to work at the restaurant.

On any slow night at The Brass Rail, my mother was able to finish work at ten p.m., and she could catch the last ferry leaving Hamilton to go to Darrell's Wharf in Warwick. One night, my mother came in very upset and mad. Her dress was ripped and bloodied, and she had been assaulted. She didn't tell us children exactly what happened, and I never questioned her, but from that point on my older brother Larry and myself were instructed to meet her every night at Darrell's Wharf and escort her home. My brother came with me for about two weeks, then he stopped, but I always made sure I was going to be there to meet her.

When she had to work late, I would take my bicycle on the ferry to Hamilton and go to "The Brass Rail" to wait until she finished. Whenever I went to The Brass Rail, I had to wait in the back of the restaurant, as I was not allowed inside the restaurant. One night while waiting for my mother, it rained so hard that the only place that I could keep dry was inside a trash can. When my mother and three other Black ladies came outside, one of the ladies said to my mother, "*He's not here!*", and my mother replied, "*He's here somewhere,*" as she knew that I would never not show up to escort her home. That is when I lifted the top to the trash can and said "*I'm here.*"

On many occasions, such as whenever my mother had to work late and would miss the last ferry to Warwick, or if my bike had a flat tire, I would race to catch the ferry back to town so I could walk home with her from Hamilton to our house to Spring Hill, which had very little street lights and was five miles. Sometimes, there was a guy named Kramer who used to drive horse and buggy carriage rides for tourists. Once in a while momma and I were walking, he would be on his way home, and we would get a ride part way from him as the stables were near Southlands to our house.

      One night while travelling on the ferry towards Hamilton to pick up my mother, in the distance I could see that the sky was bright red and realized that it was a fire. Walking up the street to The Brass Rail restaurant, I could see that The Hamilton Hotel was on fire. The Hamilton Hotel, which was up the street from the restaurant, was located on Church street, and was the first hotel in Bermuda. There appeared to be total panic, as there were people and horse and carriages scrambling to get out of Hamilton. When I found my mother amongst the crowds, she hopped on my pedal bike, sitting side saddle on the bar, and we hurried out of the City. I would peddle all the way home and whenever we came to a hill, even though my mother was only four feet ten inches, we would both have to walk over the hill, as I could not ride over it with her on the bike. That night in 1955, The Hamilton Hotel, which at that time was the largest hotel in Bermuda, burned completely to the ground. When we arrived home to Spring Hill, the fire was so vast that we could see it from there, and although it was the most frightening thing I had ever seen, I found it to also be the most exciting thing I had ever experienced.

My siblings and my mother at my wedding.

CHAPTER THREE
Whatever Happened to My Spring Hill?

Growing up on Spring Hill, everyone there was very friendly and there were quite a few elderly folks in the neighborhood who were like extended parents to us. The neighborhood children would come to the edge of our property, where there was a street light, and the boys would often talk about our future as to what we wanted to be when we grew up.

Whenever we were out mingling with one another, and saw any of the older folks walking home with bags of groceries or carrying other items, whoever spotted them first would dash off to help them with their bags. There was one elderly gentleman, who was blind and everyday he would go to The Warwick Workman's Club and have an occasional drink with his friends, and when he left the club around six-thirty p.m. every day, one of us would always guide him to his house.

Many years later, most of the original families who lived on Spring Hill had moved away, including my family, but one of my friends who was married by now had bought a house next to the "Poor house" where we had once lived. One day, he called me to ask if I could come and help him fit a new door. Later that evening, I put my tools on my scooter and went to his house and on my way, I passed about fifteen young adults who were sitting on the wall by Bright Temple Church at the foot of Spring Hill. It was about three hours later that I finished helping my friend to fit his new door, and when I left, I rode down that same hill. As I approached Bright Temple, the number of young people sitting on the wall had grown to twenty or more. Making the turn on the bend, I was surprised as I could feel rocks hitting me on my helmet, my back and my legs. By now, I was travelling along the railroad tracks speeding to get away from them, and as I was speeding, in the distance, I could see someone walking in the middle of the track with a flashlight who seemed confused as to which side they should go on, because of my wobbling from side to side.

    I chose to stay on the left side to avoid hitting this person and crashed into the cherry trees and landed on the road with my tools scattered everywhere and my scooter on top of me. After my crash, I realized the person with the flashlight was an elderly lady, and as I was lying on the ground with the scooter still on top of me, she stood over me and pointing the flashlight, kept saying " *You stupid young punk! You stupid young punk, you could have killed me, you could have killed me!*" and went off mumbling to herself " *These stupid young punks!*" I finally got up and in the darkness I searched for my tools, found them, and put them into my box and was on my way home which was on the south side of Cobb's Hill.

    As I was riding home, the lady's words kept echoing in my ears about me being a "young stupid punk," because at that time I was forty years old, and these words made me very angry, so I decided to turn around and go to the top of Cobbs Hill to an area called Ring Court, which was a back road to Spring Hill which lead to an area known as Bascome Field. It was there that I parked my bike, and took my helmet off, and from a nearby garden, I chose a spice stick which was about three and a half feet long. I then peeked around the corner and I could see the young men who had pelted me with the rocks and heard them bragging, with one saying, "*I hit *him in the back*" and another bragging about how he hit me in the head, and so on and so on.

I then pretended that I was limping along using the stick as if it were a walking cane and walked close to the wall where two of them were sitting side by side. As I walked, some of them actually moved out of the way for the 'poor elderly man' who was limping. I pretended as if I was going to walk past them, but as I got in line with them I backhanded one on his right arm and then I whacked the other one on his left arm, and I then swung and hit the third guy on his shoulder, which totally took them all by surprised. When I came down to hit the fourth guy he took off as if he were an Olympic runner, and as I looked around, I saw them all scattering away, and I was left all alone. Everyone vanished after I had whacked the three guys and after I left, before going home, I rode around the area many times from different directions and never saw a soul anywhere. As the guys of the group all scattered, there were two girls that were left behind crying out saying, "*Please don't hit us Mr., Please don't!*". I screamed out to them, "*Well GO HOME!!*" and they jumped and scattered screaming all the way to their home.

Not seeing anyone in the area, I jumped off my bike and actually went down the tracks looking for them in bushes, and although I could hear scattering in the bushes, I never saw them, because they all knew that I was a marathon runner, and the one thing they did not want, was to be caught by me and get another whooping.

Six years after my incident with the Spring Hill young boys, as I was driving out of Hamilton on my way home, a young man called out to me

"*Mr. Bean, are you going up the country?*" I pulled over and when he got in he asked me if I could give him a ride to The Warwick Workman's Club, near Spring Hill. While driving along, the young man said to me, "*Mr. Bean, you don't remember me, do you?*" and I said "*No, is there any reason that I should.*" He then continued by saying "*Remember that time you lashed me, my brother and a couple of other guys on Spring Hill.*" He then told me that I really hurt his brother and the other guys but he was not hurt as bad as they were. He further explained how that night they had waited for me and he could tell me that I drove around Spring Hill seven times and that I got off my bike and was looking for them in the bushes. He also explained to me how they had returned to "Bascome Field", because we knew that you would not come back there to look for us, and he went on to say that he told his brother and the other guys "*That man is really mad,*" so I told them, "*I'm going home*" and they all followed suit. I replied, "*Yes, I was really mad, what made you guys do that?*" He replied, "*Mr. Bean, we had nothing to do, but what we did to you wasn't the right thing, and we all learned a real lesson from you that night.*" It seems that now they all have nice jobs and are making something out of their lives. He then apologized to me, albeit six years later, and when I think about it, I feel good that these young men recognized who I was, and made something of themselves. It was a nice feeling.

CHAPTER FOUR
Our First Television

One of the biggest concerns that my mother had with us children was when television first came to Bermuda and was televised from the Kindley Air Force Base. At that time, we did not have a television, and for a while and quite often we would go to the neighbor's house which was at the bottom of Spring Hill, and stand outside on their porch and watch their television through the window. We were being extremely mindful that we had to be quiet. My mother did not like this idea, as she felt that we should be at home particularly to do our chores and homework, so she was determined to buy a television so that we would not be all over the neighborhood. I can remember the day that my mother surprised us all with a brand new television. She had not told us that she was going to buy one, and when we arrived home from school one day, there it was. At the time there was a store in Hamilton called Pearman Wallington, where my mother was able to buy a television with a down-payment of £2.10 shillings and then pay ten shillings a week.

My mother was quite stern when it came to us children doing our chores, in particular our homework, so whenever she had to go to work or some other event, she would always ask our neighbor, Mrs. Grace Simons, who was like a second mother to us, to help us with our homework. Oftentimes, Mrs. Simons would even cook a meal for us. By this time, my three oldest siblings and I were attending Purvis School, which is an elementary school. One time, when Mrs. Simons was helping me with my homework, she remembered that she had seen the same homework before, and when she pulled my books from her closet and checked, she was amazed to find out that this was the third time that I was doing the same homework. For some reason, the principal, Mrs. Gayle, and most of the teachers at Purvis School treated my family badly and gave us a very hard time. I feel that we were mistreated this way because we were looked upon as being poor, and my father had died at an early age, and my mother was raising ten children on her own. Unfortunately, as a single mother raising ten children, she could never attend any of the PTA meetings, as she had to work two or three jobs to put food on the table and clothing on the backs of her children, and I think this was part of the reason the teachers looked down or didn't really care for us.

  An example of one of the ways in which the teachers mistreated myself and my siblings; were in the case of my oldest sister Violeta who was the most talented and intelligent above all the students who were in her class. The school always chose her for her talents in singing, sports, and acting. Whenever concerts were being had, they also chose her as the lead singer. She performed several times at the Opera House Theatre on behalf of the school, and later became Bermuda's top artist and performer- entertaining in all the major hotels and nightclubs. She also recorded two albums, Early Autumn by the Bermuda Sounds & My Shining Hour which was a solo album.

  During Violeta's last year at Purvis School she had won the first Scholarship put forward by The Warwick Workman's Club for being the top student at Purvis School. Although the principal, Mrs. Gayle and Violeta's homeroom teacher, Mrs. Raynor knew Violeta had won the scholarship fair and square, they intentionally did not give it to her, but gave it to another student, who was the same age as Violeta, but who came from a wealthy family. When one of the popular teacher's, Mrs. Blackett found out that Violeta did not receive the scholarship, she confronted Mrs. Gayle and Mrs. Raynor to question why Violeta, who was the clear winner, was not given the scholarship. After having no success with them, she went directly to The Warwick Workman's Club and told the President how Violeta Bean was the top student, hands down and how the Principal and Mrs. Raynor denied awarding her with the Scholarship. Their reasoning was that she was too young to receive it, therefore she would not be able go on to higher learning because her family could not afford to send her to the Berkeley Institute. Once Mrs. Blackett had explained Violeta's situation to the President of the Club, the Club then gave Violeta a personal Scholarship and she was able to attend the Berkeley Institute where she excelled in her schooling and left there as a Top Student.

    Other ways in which the teachers at Purvis School mistreated us, was for two years I had come first in class marks, but each year I was held back as well as my brother Larry. Every time I was in Mrs. Trott's class and she was writing a sum on the blackboard, before she finished, I would always shout out the answer, and although she knew I was right, she would get extremely upset and even came to my desk and lifted up the top because she thought I had the answer written on a piece of paper in the desk. When she did not find anything in the desk, she would make me stand up because she thought I was sitting on the answer. Once, she even sat me in a corner with my back to the class and put a DUNCE cap on my head.

Shortly after this incident, she called my brother Larry who happened to be in the same class with me, although he was one year older, to the front of the class and made him a Prefect and told him not to let anyone in or out of the class until she gets back. There was a young girl in our class named Diane, who happened to be the principal's daughter, and she did not like the idea that the teacher had asked my brother to monitor the door, so she went up to him and told him that she had to go to the bathroom. He refused to let her go out and she made every effort to push the door open and for a while there was a tug-of-war between the two of them with the door. When he finally managed to push the door shut, somehow the door smashed her fingers. Well, Diane screamed so loud that her mother and all the teachers came running. The principal, dragging my brother by the ear, took him to the office and beat him with a cane, and as he refused to cry, she kept on beating him and this left horrendous welts all over his body, which swelled up badly.

When Larry returned to the class, as further punishment, Mrs. Trott told him to go into the closet. After about fifteen minutes, Mrs. Trott asked one of the boys whose name was Hilgrove to go and get Larry from the closet. When the boy opened the door, he did not see Larry, so he went back to his desk. After about five minutes, Mrs. Trott realized that Larry was not at his desk, and she said to Hilgrove *"Didn't I tell you to get Larry out of the closet?"* and Hilgrove replied *"But Mrs. Trott he is not in there."* Mrs. Trott then shouted to him to go back to the closet to get him. Again, Hilgrove went back to look in the closet and then walked back to his seat, and said *"Mrs. Trott, Larry is not there!"* Mrs. Trott then got up and went to the closet herself, but did not see Larry and she then asked the whole class if anyone had seen Larry come out of the closet, and we all replied, "*No, Mrs. Trott.*"

Mrs. Trott stormed out of the class and went to the Head Office and asked Mrs. Gayle if all of the older boys could go and look for Larry, and said that "*No one is going home until we find him.*" The principal, Mrs. Gayle came to the classroom herself to check the closet but she did not see Larry in the closet, or at all, and closed the door. Mrs. Gayle then asked the classroom if anyone had seen him, and everyone replied "*No, Mrs. Gayle*" so she left and you could tell that she was completely upset, because she knew she had beaten him badly. Upon returning to the classroom and being seated at her desk, Mrs. Trott suddenly heard drum beats and asked "*Where is that noise coming from?*" and one of the students said "*from the closet,*" and that was when she looked in there, and there was Larry, sitting beating drums! Mrs. Trott asked him, "*Where have you been, boy?*" and with a straight face, he said "*In the closet,*" and she shouted back at him "*No you were not!*" and he responded by saying "*Mrs. Trott, you just opened the door and I'm here.*" Mrs. Trott knew full well that he was not in the closet when she looked, and this upset her so much that she shouted at him to "*Go back to your desk,*" and she then dismissed the class. Mrs. Trott was so angry that she just went and sat at her desk and cried. After the missing episode with Larry, Mrs. Trott never punished anyone else by sending them in the closet.

Every afternoon when school was dismissed, the first thing Larry and I did was take our shoes and socks off, as we did not want to wear them out because we knew that our mother could not afford to buy us new ones. We used to take a shortcut home across the Belmont Golf Course, and while walking home one day, I decided to ask Larry where he was when they looked in the closet. He told me that he had climbed up on the shelves, opened the trap door, climbed through the ceiling, and then closed the trap door behind him. He then walked through the ceiling above most of the classrooms and then back through the trap door to our classroom. That is when he started to beat the drums. Earlier in my story I had mentioned that when Mrs. Simons had realized I was repeating my homework for the past two years, she took my brother and I to her sister, Delton Tucker who was the Principal at the Southampton Glebe School, and she immediately enrolled us there, where we both excelled as Top Students. I did not stay in school as I eventually was discouraged overall, and left at the age of thirteen to pick up work to help the family.

CHAPTER FIVE
Male Predators

There are some things in life that were never explained to me by my parents. Predatory behavior by women and men was one of them. It is not a conversation that one wants to talk about, but considering what can happen to children, girls AND boys, it is something that folks should discuss and warn children of.

One day, after swimming with some of my friends at a place called Caine's Rock, which was next to a restaurant called The Sea Venture located at Darrell's Wharf on Harbour Road in Warwick, my friends left to go home. I decided I would stay behind to do some fishing. While I was there alone, a guy who I knew approached me, didn't say anything, and started to pull my trunks down. I was shocked, and when I realized what he was attempting to do, I gave him one hard push backward, and he landed flat on his back on the sharp jagged rocks on the water's edge. I was winding up my fishing line to get out of there as fast as I could, and I looked back to see that he was still lying there in severe pain. The next time I saw him he had his arm in a cast, had one crutch, and was bandaged from head to toe. Nothing was ever said about that incident.

There was another experience that I had at the Warwick Workman's Club. I had to go to the Men's Room which was two flights down in what seemed to be a dungeon. I walked into the bathroom, went into a cubicle, and before I could even lock the cubicle door, it was being pushed open. It was being pushed so hard that I could not close it- it was then I realized a man was trying to enter the same cubicle- not by accident. I allowed the door to open right up so that I could go out, but he kept pushing his way to come in and it was then that I put my foot against the toilet bowl and gave him one great shove- pushing him back so hard and fast it was like a cannon being fired. He landed across the bathroom with the lower part of his body hitting the sink hard and the back of his head smashing into the mirror which shattered. Blood was running down from the back of his head, and he ended up in a sitting position completely knocked out while I ran out of there as fast as my legs could carry me.

    Later on, I heard members of the Club say how there was blood on the mirror in the Men's Room, and later they realized who had the accident in the men's room, but they never knew what had actually happened in there.

CHAPTER SIX
The Manager's Wife and Her Poodle

In 1956 at the age of thirteen, I was working as an apprentice at the Carpenter Shop at The Elbow Beach Hotel. An apprentice had to do odd jobs like keep the shop clean by sweeping the floors, fix broken locks and fix jammed windows. I had a few practice jobs and due to my handiness I was able to do larger jobs quickly along the way. On one particular occasion, I was called to the eastern cottage, where the Hotel Manager and his wife lived. I was called to fix a broken lock, which I was very good at. The housekeeper who met me at the door was my neighbor and the mother of three of my best friends. She showed me the broken lock, but while explaining things to me, the managers' wife's dog, a black poodle, just kept barking and barking, until I gave it a stern arm throw with my finger pointing to the ground. The dog immediately shut up and went to the ground in a lying position. I did not realize the manager's wife was watching me, and to my surprise, saw when I pointed my finger at her dog. She asked me, "*What did you do to my dog?*" I replied "*I had demanded that he shut up and he did.*" After finishing the lock, I left. Three days later a call came through the Carpenter Shop from the housekeeper of eastern cottage, and she told me that the manager's wife specifically asked for me to come and walk her dog.

After the first day of walking the dog, it became a regular thing, and for the next two weeks from eleven a.m. to noon this became one of my duties, which I thoroughly enjoyed, as I had trained the dog to do many tricks. I hadn't realized that the manager's wife was watching me when I was teaching the dog to do these tricks, until one day, I happened to see her standing at a window watching me. This made me feel very jittery and uncomfortable. A few weeks later, the housekeeper called the carpenter shop and told me that the manager's wife would like to change the time for walking the dog from eleven a.m. to two p.m. Upon arriving at the cottage at two p.m. to take the dog for his walk, I saw the housekeeper leave, as this was her usual time to finish for the day.

After walking the dog for an hour, when I returned to the house, the manager's wife asked me if I would bring the dog inside, which was very strange; because, the dog would normally go in on his own. Once I got inside she gave me a glass of orange juice and after I drank it and was ready to leave, she grabbed my hand and led me to what I believe was the dog's bedroom. She then pushed me down on the bed, took advantage of me, and threatened me to not tell anyone because if I tell anyone, she said, I would get locked up and lose my job. Later when I thought about the incident, I realized that the reason the manager's wife had changed the time was due to the fact that her husband had left the island to go on a business trip on behalf of the hotel. When she threatened me about losing my job and being locked up, I could not help but to think of a friend of mine who lived in my neighborhood and was having an affair for many months with a White woman whose husband was a Marine at the United States Air Force Base. Two and three times a week, my friend who was three years older than me, used to go into the bushes with this woman for what I can only imagine at the time was sex. One day it was raining and the woman took him in the house, and her husband came home early and they got caught. The woman screamed "*RAPE!*", and my friend ended up getting twenty years in jail, so that's all I could think of when the manager's wife threatened me.

The next day, I received a call from the housekeeper asking if I would come and walk the dog at eleven a.m. When I arrived at the cottage, the housekeeper noticed that I was nervous, and asked me, "*If everything was alright.*" I said, "*Yes,*" and then took the dog for a walk but when I came back, the housekeeper noticed that I was not comfortable and I was not myself. She then asked me "*If anything had happened?*" and I nervously replied "*No.*" A few days later while playing marbles in her yard, she called me aside and questioned me again about whether something had happened with the manager's wife, because she had a strong feeling that something had happened and she really wanted to know, but I could not tell her, because I felt I would get locked up and lose my job. She then said to me, that "*If I ever had to walk the dog in the afternoon, she would wait for me, to make sure I was safe.*" Every time thereafter when I walked the dog in the afternoon she waited for me as a result of that incident.

Because my neighbor waited for me, the manager's wife never had the opportunity to assault me again, but for many years after that, whenever I saw a policeman, especially in my neighborhood, I would go and hide because I would always feel that they were after me.

CHAPTER SEVEN
College Kids

After the horrific experience that I had with the manager's wife and her dog, four months later in March of 1957 was the starting month of most colleges' Spring Break, and when the island accommodated "College Kids" by the thousands. Elbow Beach Hotel at that time would only take in girls, unless the boy's parents were staying at the hotel.

One day while working in the carpenter shop, we received a worksheet order to go to room 546 which was a penthouse suite located on the fifth floor to fix a broken window, and at that time the suite had seven female college students occupying it. A senior worker, who was teaching me about the trades of the jobs and myself went to the room, and after accessing the window, he said that I could do the job myself, and left me there. Off he went to do another job.

In order to fix the problem, I had to position myself by sitting on the sill with my upper body on the outside of the window and my feet resting inside on the floor. While in this position and focusing on the job, all of a sudden, I felt hands on both sides of the lower part of my body and another hand behind my back to support me from falling. As I jumped up one of the female students said, "*We won't let you fall.*" I was so shocked that I couldn't even speak, and I immediately slid back into the room. The girls took advantage of me. About a half hour after the incident, a knock came on the door, and everyone scrambled. Four of them ran into the bathroom and one made sure that my pants were up before she ran off. When the senior carpenter entered the room, the only people in there was the girl that opened the door; one sitting on the couch and one on a chair. Without suspecting anything the senior carpenter checked the window, gave his approval, and I picked up my tools and walked out, knowing that I would not tell a soul what had happened to me, in fear that the girls would call out "*Rape!*" and I would lose my job and go to jail.

CHAPTER EIGHT
Blaming Blacks for Crimes They Did Not Commit

In August of 1956 at the age of thirteen, I started working in the Carpenter Shop at The Elbow Beach Hotel. In those days, when one started employment, it was the usual practice to be paid one week later, and we were given a half day off on Saturday's. In order to make some extra money, I used to go to Darrell's Wharf on the Saturday to perform for the tourists by dancing and diving off the dock with the greatest of skills. To get the most applause and money, you had to be fancy with your dive with somersaults and backwards flips, jackknife and the swanee with your arms out like a bird diving down to the water. This was a self-taught skill that impressed the tourists.

On my first Saturday off, while I was on my way to Darrell's Wharf, I was passing the Warwick Academy playing field, which was about one hundred yards from my house. On the field, there were five little White boys playing football. When I passed by, they kicked the ball out to me and when I kicked it back, they asked me to come and play with them to make two even teams- three against three. After about an hour of playing, two white policemen appeared. I felt that one of the parents or one of the White folks on the hill had called them to say that there was a little Black boy on the Warwick Academy school field playing with the White boys. The thing is, Warwick Academy was not a school that allowed Black children, in fact it wasn't until 1962 that it was integrated, so a Black child on <u>this</u> field was not allowed.

When the policemen came up to us, we had gathered together, and then a policeman with a large handlebar moustache, said in his broken English "*Darkie, what you doing on this field?*" and before I could speak, the White boys said to the policeman "*He is our friend and we asked him to come and play with us,*" but the policeman ignored what they said and again asked me, "*Darkie what you doing on this field?*". Before I could answer he grabbed me by the shoulder and also by the cuff of my shorts and threw me in the police jeep. When he threw me, the seats, which were made of metal, were scorching hot, and I tried to sit on my hands to prevent burning my butt. As they drove off, they started to accuse me of many things, which I knew nothing about, and I kept denying the accusations.

They drove me to the police station in Hamilton and when they arrived, they wound up the windows and took the handles off. They locked up the jeep and went into the station, leaving me in the hot jeep without any air. While I was sitting there, there were many people outside staring at me, as if I was a trapped animal in a cage. After a while, I was having difficulty breathing, but of course I could not wind down the windows as the handles were removed. After what seemed to be an eternity, I tried to put my head between my legs thinking I could get some air, but that was impossible and I eventually blacked out.

When I came to, I found myself on the floor and was very, very dizzy, gasping for air. I could not move my body, because it was so weak, and I then realized that the doors of the jeep were open, and the two policemen were standing outside of the jeep, appearing to be getting in. They were standing there, just talking to one another, but with the door open I could feel my body getting stronger with the air being let in. I believe that when the policemen saw me lying on the floor, they probably thought that I was sleeping, not realizing that I was probably near death from suffocation. They just went on talking to each other for about ten minutes or more about whatever plans they had in mind for me, because they never took me into the station to be charged with anything that they had accused me of.

Once my body fully recovered, I was able to sit back on the hot bench, and it was then I realized that my face, arms and legs were burnt from lying on the hot metal floor. Once the policemen got into the jeep, they said to me, "*Darkie, you're going with us.*" They then drove me all through the back of town, which I had never been before, and then drove me to what I now believe was Orange Valley which was nothing but trees at the time, and was pitch black, although it was daylight. As they were driving me in these parts unknown, all I could do was think of my mother, and I started to become concerned. I knew that my mother knew that I would never do anything to get into trouble and she thinks I am at Darrell's Wharf diving but instead the police had me driving around to places I had no knowledge of at thirteen years of age.

One of my other concerns was that I did not want to lose my job, which she had just gotten for me at Elbow Beach, and although I was only thirteen at that time I was the sole breadwinner and was the only child out of ten helping my mother to support the family. Once we left the Orange Valley area, the policemen then drove me to the Brighton Hill area, and I could hear them talking on their hand radio to someone at the station, saying that "*We have a dark kid, with a polo shirt, khaki shorts and no shoes,*" and after a brief pause, they responded to what was being said to them, and they replied, "*We will do that.*" They then drove to the foot of Brighton Hill in front of what I now know to be Ariel Sands, and stopped and told me to" *GET OUT AND GO HOME!*" and I said to them "*Sir, I don't know where home is, because I have never been here before.*" They then shouted louder "*GET OUT!*" and I jumped out of the jeep as fast as I could.

When I got out of the jeep, I was afraid and was shaking all over, as there were a lot of White people standing around looking at me and they heard the way the policemen screamed at me to "*GET OUT*" which drew their attention to me even more. I think they probably wondered why the police had put me out there; as this was an area in Bermuda that Blacks were not allowed in at the time. The policemen then drove off in an easterly direction, so I then walked in the opposite direction for about one hundred yards. As I was walking, a taxi went speeding by, slammed brakes and reversed back to me. The first thing that came out of his mouth was, "*Beanie, what the hell you doing down here?*" He then asked, "*Do you know that you could be locked up for being in this area?*" I replied, "*The police brought me here and left me!*" The driver, who ironically happened to be my neighbor, then said to me "*Get in this car!*"

As we drove towards Tee Street, we saw a paddy wagon speeding in the direction that I had just left. The taxi driver then said to me, "*They are going to get you, that's why they left you where they did- they know that no Blacks should be in the area, and they would arrest you for wandering* abroad and stealing. They would lock you up for nine months to three years!" The taxi driver then explained to me that the reason they put me in that area was because a lot of the English and Scottish policemen stole things themselves and they knew that they could pick up any Black person, anywhere, anytime and put them in the scene of the crime. Many Black people were blamed for a lot of their dirty work.

    The taxi driver then drove me to Darrell's Wharf, where I was fortunate enough to catch the last boat with tourists on it and I made £2.00, which I gladly took home to my mother. While dressing for Sunday school the next day, my mother noticed the blisters on my face, arms and legs, and said to me, "*Didn't I tell you to stay out of the sun.*" She then put calamine lotion on all of my blisters, and I breathed a big sigh of relief, because I did not have to tell her what had actually happened to me. After putting the lotion on, she said to me "*You cannot go to Sunday school with all those blisters on your body.*"

    Many years after the horrific experience of being in the police jeep with locked windows and getting no air, I still have all kinds of dreams and nightmares of suffocating and gasping for air. No matter what type of dream it is, I always wake up gasping for air and sometimes kicking and punching quite violently, which can be very disturbing and upsetting to my wife. Many times, my wife had to jump and roll out of bed to avoid being struck by me unintentionally.

CHAPTER NINE
The Peeping Tom Confession

Every evening from Monday to Friday, I would visit my neighbor, Mr. Bascome, who was building a new home next to his homestead, and Mr. Bascome was teaching me masonry work. While working from eight o'clock to nine o'clock we would listen to classical music on the radio, and from nine o'clock to ten o'clock we would listen to the English stories like "Scotland Yard," "Dragnet," and other mystery stories. Many nights when I left Mr. Bascome's house I would see a White man either running or walking by.

On many occasions, my mother used to send me to Nabor Edness's grocery store on Ord Road to buy kerosene oil. Kerosene oil was used to light lamps as well as the stove at the time. One night, while on my way home from the shop, I heard someone running behind me and the person was breathing heavily as they ran straight past me. I could feel the thumping of his footsteps, as he was a very large man. I recognized this man as being White, and as I mentioned, I had seen him running quite often, but never knew where he was running to and from. A few seconds later another White man came running up to me, stopped, and asked if I saw a man running this way. I told him that he had run straight through Tribe Road No. 1. As I made a right turn, I could hear heavy breathing coming from the bushes, and I realized that the first man did not go straight through, but was lying in the bushes, and the man chasing him would not have heard the heavy breathing because he had kept running straight through Tribe Road.

The next day I went to Mr. Edness's shop with my collection of mineral and rum bottles to buy cupcakes and soda. In those days, you could buy a lot of goodies with the exchange of bottles. When I arrived at the shop, there were two or three policemen there checking out the people coming into the shop, and that was when I heard that a White girl in the neighborhood had been raped. I had learned there was a Black man called "Sheik", who was probably in his fifties, who lived not too far from the grocery store, had been arrested for the rape of this young girl. When the neighborhood people heard that Sheik was arrested, they were angry, because although this gentleman did drink a lot, he kept to himself, and he would go around the neighborhood helping people with cutting their grass, so the neighborhood felt they knew that he would never hurt anyone.

When the case came up in court, the little girl could not identify Sheik as the rapist, because he was midnight black, and she knew that the man that raped her was a White man. When Sheik appeared in court, to my surprise, the White man that I often saw running at nights, testified that he saw Sheik in the area the night of the rape, but Sheik only lived a hundred yards from the store and every night he would go there to buy his liquor. The lawyers forced Sheik to sign a confession, telling him that he would not have to do too much time in jail, and as he was an uneducated Black man, he signed the confession. The Court sentenced this innocent man to more than twenty years in jail for a crime he did not commit. Shortly after Sheik had been arrested and accused for a crime he did not commit, I started to put two and two together, and remembered the night I had seen this White man running and the other White man chasing him, I realized that the young girl who had been raped, was the second man's daughter and the first man hiding in the trees was a Peeping Tom. It also dawned on me, as I mentioned earlier, that quite often I would see this man running at night. The man who testified against Sheik was the actual peeping Tom.

Some years after the rape incident, when I was between the age of sixteen-seventeen, and had saved enough money to put down on a motorbike, I went to a well-known garage and to my shock, I recognized the owner as being the man that was referred to as the "Peeping Tom." I was even more shocked, because while I was in the garage making the down payment on my bike, I saw two boys there who were my good friends, and realized that this man was in fact their father.

Many years later in his old age, Mr. Peeping Tom was hospitalized and while on his deathbed, he confessed that he had raped the girl, and admitted that Sheik was innocent!

CHAPTER TEN
My Part-Time Night Job

At one time, Elbow beach had a problem with "Peeping Toms". Along the property grounds there were pole lamp lights, about thirty-five of them, and folks would climb up the pole and turn out the lights to be able to look into hotel guests' windows. There was a buddy who was the electrician there, and he asked me if I wanted a part-time night job. The job was to go around the whole property, and if there were any lights that were burnt out or turned off, and replace them. Since I was walking through the property, I would hear all sorts of things scurrying and scrambling in the bushes, and I heard crackling leaves and sticks. Truth be told it was kind of scary. At this time, I had a few German Shepherd dogs at home, and the next night, I brought the dogs, Rusty, Sandy and Tora with me. The Security officer saw me and said, "*Hey, where are you going with them dogs?*" I told him I was walking the property to check the lights, and wanted them with me. He said, "*Go ahead, just keep them on the leash, and while you are at it, on the public Tribe Road, you will find some motorbikes parked up there, try to get their license numbers.*" Sure thing, and off I went.

Since I was walking with the dogs, I was not scared anymore, and not long after we got on walking, the dog's ears perked up. People were scrambling through the bushes, and Rusty was barking at a person who went up a tree. The man was afraid to get down as he thought the dogs were going to bite him. He kept screaming, "*Don't let the dog bite me,*" and I said, "*he isn't going to bite you, but you have to get out that tree.*" Once he got down, I noticed this guy was dressed in a suit and sneakers, and I asked him, "*which one of these bikes is yours?*". He told me, and I said, "*Look, you know you are not supposed to be here, now get off the property and look, I am turning over this list to the Police, so if I see the bike back here you are going to court*". There was another guy who, after the dogs spotted him and they started barking, went up a fire escape, and tried to climb to the roof. I started yelling at him, "*You better get down from there, I am telling you once, and then I am sending the dogs up*" he came down, also afraid the dogs were going to get at him because they were barking mad. I told him the same thing, that if he is found around there again the Police will be called.

There were a few times when I went around the property and caught some people, even some of the foreign guest workers up in the trees peeping in on the guests, and found out that they were the ones putting out the lights. One guy didn't even get a chance to come down off the pole, as the dogs ran up to him. I told him, "*Get down from there, but before you come down, turn back on that light!*" Another time, as I was walking the property, the dogs came upon a woman who was in the bushes, who seemed to be looking for something. I yelled to her, "*Ma'am, what are you doing?*" She responded by saying, "*I'm just looking for someone*". I asked "*Who?*" She said, "*My husband*". I can say this, after I made a few rounds with my dogs, for at least two years, Elbow Beach had no problems with peeping toms due to Sandy, Rusty, and Tora.

CHAPTER ELEVEN
Desperate for A Babysitter

Every Sunday morning my siblings and I, together with the neighborhood children, would walk from Spring Hill down to Cobbs Hill to the Gospel Chapel for Sunday School for ten o'clock service. Immediately after Sunday School, we would go upstairs for the eleven a.m. church service. After the church service we would then go home and have lunch and we then had to be ready for Mrs. Simons to pick us up to take us to her Sunday School which was on the corner of Middle and Manse Road in Paget for three o'clock in the afternoon. We would then go back to Mrs. Simons or one of her sister's homes which was on Dudley Hill for dinner and then back to Mrs. Simon's church for seven p.m. until nine p.m. The events of going to Sunday school and church all day started at the age of eight and continued until the age of thirteen, when I started to work and began to take control of my own time.

I remember that Mrs. Simons had an apartment in her house, and a White couple who were from Alabama lived there. Back then, the US. Naval Base has rented several homes from Black Bermudians who had extra apartments for their White servicemen. This couple that was being housed in Mrs. Simons house was very prejudiced, always referred to us as "Niggas." This couple owned a German Shepard dog who they had trained to dislikes "Niggas," and we all were very afraid of it. The husband use to tell me and the other little boys stories of how in Alabama they would hang "Niggas" and how the dogs would be ripping their bodies apart. As he was telling us children these stories, you could tell that he really enjoyed it and it was as if he was very proud of how they treated the Black people in America. They were not friendly to the Black neighbors at all.

On one occasion when the Naval Base was having an event and this couple wanted to go, but could not find a babysitter. They had tried all around the neighborhood, but because of the way they treated the Blacks no one wanted to babysit for them. As a last resort, they asked my mother and she sent two of my older sisters to their home. After my sisters had babysat, the couple told my mother that one of them had stolen something, and my mother told them that was not the case, and that they would not be babysitting for them again because she knows that they did not steal anything. Well, shortly after this incident, an event celebrating the 4th of July came up for the personnel at the Base and again, they needed a babysitter. Ironically they told my mother that they had found the "thing" that went missing and could the girls babysit for them again. My mother told them "*No!*" and they begged and pleaded with her, saying they would pay my sisters double, so my mother reluctantly said "*Yes*" and sent me along with one of my sisters. We never had them complain again.

CHAPTER TWELVE
Bermuda Hospitality

Back in the day, we as hotel workers put so much into the hospitality and service we gave our guests, we did everything we could do to make their stay a pleasurable one. If a worker was walking through the lobby, and a guest needed assistance, someone would do a 180-degree turnaround in any direction to go and assist the visitor to the best of our ability. _This is the hospitality Bermuda became known for._ It seems that very few of the hotel managers ever really realized how much their workers were putting into the hospitality towards their guests, in fact, they had no clue that we workers were actually competing against each other to give the best service to our guests and to show the true beauty of Bermuda that made visitors come back each and every year. What did it mean to give our best? Along with our regular everyday duties, we went the extra mile with a smile. If you were an entertainer, you got it all. The management did give out little service awards from the government, but the true Bermuda spirit was constantly shown on every level in the hotel, by us hospitality workers both men and women.

One year, while working on the beach, the hotel had a convention group of about 500 people staying for a week from New Jersey, USA. While the convention group was there for the week, as a beach attendant, they would often come to the beach and ask me what is there to do on the Island. They wanted to browse around the island, go on tours to different places, and see what is fun to do. The foreign guest workers would mostly give tourists information to go see the touristy stuff, The Crystal Caves, The

Lighthouse, etc. Those are all wonderful places, but some folks wanted to see the local views. As a beach attendant, I would get these questions thousands of times a day, and would want to give them some of the best things to do in Bermuda besides swimming.

Back then, in Bermuda, every Thursday was a half day for most workers. Everything shut down, and there were weddings held, football being played, boat sailing, fishing, and Thursday's cricket. Now, Cup match is the largest cricket game between the East and West in Bermuda, but there are Central County, Western County and the Eastern County Games that also happen. The largest of those games was the Eastern County Games, which are the second largest cricket game in all of Bermuda. It is a series that goes on between four teams in the East; St. David's, Flats, Cleveland County, and Bailey's Bay on home field and away privileges. If St. David's wins the cup, their club keeps it down their yard (their field), until it is lost to the opposing team.

At that time, very few local Whites patronized our sports. On the half day Thursdays, the White foreign workers typically went sailing or did some other activity, mainly just headed to the beach. Meanwhile, if the Eastern County Games were playing, then all of the Black hospitality workers from domestic workers, bellman's, busboys, and bartenders all were going to the games. Since the convention guests wanted to see the "Real Bermuda", we decided we were going to take a few of them each in our cars to experience the games. The workers, including myself, took about six or so guests to the game in each of our cars.

Once I arrived with the convention guests, they saw the big crowds and got excited. Some had no idea what cricket was, but they saw all the people and the food area, and a part where folks were playing Crown & Anchor and wanted to be a part of this. They were also really excited, as they saw lots of their fellow colleagues enjoying themselves too. In the food area, there was a place called Dolly's Kitchen. Dolly had fish chowder, conch stew, muscle pie, peas and rice, mac and cheese, fish and chips, BBQ chicken, and other soups and Bermuda salads. There was one guy who was tasting all the foods, and he ate five bowls of fish chowder. Well, Dolly said the sixth must be free! All the Bermudians that were there were excited to see these new guests and were making them comfortable by explaining the game to them play by play, offering their seats, and telling them which foods they had to try. The guests were in a safe environment, and all the convention guests had such a phenomenal time, that this was all they could talk about when they returned to the hotel and when they headed home to NJ the following day.

One day, about five weeks later as I was carrying about fifteen umbrellas off the beach, a woman was looking on to the beach and called out, "*Hey, who is Rene?*"
I replied, "*I am.*"
"*Come quick, I found him, bring the camera.*" she said
Now, not knowing what the commotion is about, my knees were about to buckle, and my heart was skipping a beat. I am saying to myself, "*Now, what did I do wrong, and why is there a camera?*"

A woman came up to me, "*Hi, I am Ms. Murdock, your name is Rene, right?*"

I answered, "*Yes*".

She said, "*Your name is written on this paper here, can we sit down and talk?*"

I replied, "*I have to speak to my manager, Mickey Caines about it,*" but when I spoke to Mickey, he said go ahead.

Ms. Murdock said, "*I have a list of names of some very special people here in this book, including yours. Do you know any of these people? Can you help me find them?*" In the book, I saw my name written down, as well as the names of my colleagues who, along with me, took some of the convention guests to the County Games a few weeks ago. There was Gladys, who was in housekeeping, and Cleveland, who was a talented elevator man along with others that I knew. She could see I was hesitant, so she further explained, "*I work for this company who just had a convention here a few weeks ago, and did you all take some people to some festival?*"

"*Well, it is not a festival, it is a Cricket game on the island...*"

"*Yes, well we heard about all these different foods and all these wonderful people at this game, and am wondering if you can tell me exactly when this game is happening next year? This is all the folks have been talking about for the past weeks, so much that my boss has sent me down here to find out when it is again so we can come back again next year and experience this festival that everyone has been talking about.*" Ms. Murdock explained.

"*I don't know exactly when it will happen,*" I explained.

Ms. Murdock asked, "*Is it possible you can find out while I am here? I am here for 3 days.*"
"*Sure, I can find out when the Eastern County Games are happening next year, I can speak to the clubs.*"
Ms. Murdock then said, "*Is it possible for you to help me find these people? Are you available tomorrow at three pm? I want to take all of your photos as you all made such an impression on our workers. They would be so happy that we found you all.*" I told her where she can find the folks on the list, and explained I will be available tomorrow at three pm.

    The next day, when I get up to the hotel, I see these White guys and girls in maids and other uniforms, which they are typically not in. These were all foreign staff in the hotel, dressed up here for the picture. There were even Bellmen in Black people's uniforms, and these positions were only held by Blacks at the time. I was the only Black person in the room. Ms. Murdock came in, "*Oh Rene, you are the first one here*". She did not see where the other Black folks from her list were, as she met them the day before, and told them about the photo as well.

    When Ms. Murdock went to look for the manager, she asked him, "*Where is Gladys, where is Cleveland?*" The manager told her "*Ma'am, we cannot use all these Black people in our advertising, we have some other staff here for you to photograph.*" She says, "*Mr. Manager, these folks were not the people that made my people happy. The workers like Rene, Cleveland, and Gladys were the people that made my people happy, and these were the people we were coming back to see next year. I specifically came here to find the folks like Gladys whose spirit made our workers feel so welcomed while here, and we all want to come back here next year, to be amongst all the beautiful people of Bermuda. All these beautiful people who did so much for our five hundred employees and you send me these imposters?"* She cursed the manager out.

The manager stood his ground and still said, "*Ms. Murdock, we cannot use Black people in our advertising.*" Well, she told her photographer "*We are getting out of here! It is a shame, because **they** made Bermuda something special for us, those folks made it special.*" It truly was shameful, because that company never came back to Bermuda and took their business of over five hundred people elsewhere.

CHAPTER THIRTEEN
Beautiful Translucent Bubble

On any beautiful sunny day in Bermuda, with sparkling blue calm waters, and a beach full of swimmers, as beautiful as it is- this scene can change with a quickness and all of a sudden, you can hear someone screaming, and the whole beach seems to panic. Being a lifeguard at Elbow Beach, I had to be prepared for anything that was going on, and had an idea of what was happening there, so, I immediately jumped into the water to swim out to the swimmer. I gripped the woman swimmer, who was caught up in the tentacles of a Man-of-War. She being in a panicked state, flailing and moving aimlessly about, caused the tentacles of the Man-of-War to wrap also around me. A Man-of-War resembles a jellyfish and can get as large as your fists, with tentacles as much as six feet long. The tentacles work in a way to sting and immobilize its prey, which are fish for consumption. As a lifeguard, and watching the behavior of tourists in the waters, many are mesmerized by the beautiful translucent bubble that is atop the water and it is very deceptive as to what lies beneath is a danger to them.

After bringing her to shore I had to remove all of the tentacles with a towel and vinegar, and these tentacles covered much of her upper body. Once the lady was relaxed, and I had removed all of the tentacles, she told me how she saw this beautiful bubble floating in the water, and her curiosity got the best of her. She said she swam toward it and touched the Man-of-War, not knowing what it was. My main concern as a lifeguard was to rescue her, make sure she was alright, not panicked, and comfortable. Also, I needed to give her instructions on what would be happening next to her body as a result of the sting. It was at that point that I told her that I was used to being stung, and I explained to her a couple of things:

1. The pain would be intense for at least 3 to 4 hours.
2. During the 3 hours of pain, she would evidently feel numbness from the armpit towards the neck, and that indicates a good sign the pain is getting ready to stop within the next 30 to 40 minutes.
3. The welts that are left from the tentacles will dry up like a scab, and these scabs can last from one week to upwards of a year.

For additional information that I have gathered throughout the years see the addendum at the back of this book.

CHAPTER FOURTEEN
When You Don't Listen, You Learn the Hard Way

As a lifeguard at Elbow Beach some days you would see so many Man-of-Wars in the waters. I would tell the guest that it was not safe for them to swim, and while most were accommodating, many did not come all the way to Bermuda not to swim. One particular day, there were some guests who came to the beach with their snorkeling gear, and I informed them that it would not be safe for them to go snorkeling, as there were too many Man-of-Wars in the water, and they would not be able to see them on the surface. There were about hundreds of Man-of-Wars in the water that day. I went about my duties, and later, I noticed a couple, who I had just told about the dangers of swimming, pick up their gear and go off to the public side of Elbow Beach, which is to the west between a beach called Coral Beach and Elbow. Within the next hour, the woman of the pair was rushed back to me by at least six other swimmers. When I saw her, I could not believe my eyes, as she had so many welts on her that it appeared that she had been stung by at least two Man-of-Wars.

I immediately asked her "*Why did you go snorkeling when I had told you that it would be too dangerous out there?*" She replied that "*She thought that it would be safe to swim on the next beach.*" I slowly pulled each tentacle from her body with a towel, and after the tentacles were off, I put vinegar on the welts and I told her that she would be in pain for the next four hours. I also told her that she would experience numbness on the inner thighs of both legs, and also from her armpit up towards the neck. I explained that the numbness was a good sign, because after that all the pain would stop within the next thirty to forty minutes.

About two hours after attending to the lady, she returned to me trembling and asked about going to the hospital because she was still in so much pain, particularly on her legs. It was then I noticed that that area was very red, and I said to her "*That looks like someone had rubbed sand on it.*" and she replied "*Yes, they had!*" I told her that rubbing the sand does nothing but irritate the skin, and does not help. I also told her that it was nothing that the hospital could do, unless they put her to sleep for three to four hours to not feel the pain, and that it would cost her quite a bit of money to stay in the hospital for that amount of time. Three to four hours later, the lady came to me again in a happy mood, as she was no longer in pain and told me that everything that I had told her would happen, had actually happened, and in the order that I had told her. I then explained to her that although the pain was gone, the scabs would remain there for a week to possibly up to a year. At the end of the day, I was happy that she finally did listen to what I had to say, and had she listened earlier to the warning, she wouldn't have had to suffer as she did.

CHAPTER FIFTEEN
Now You Know What Pain Feels Like

There would be days I would often have difficulty with keeping the hotel staff from being on the guest section of the beach. Staff members were not allowed on the guest section of the beach because if something happens between a worker and a guest, it doesn't reflect well on the hotel. Guests can and will make a complaint to the managers and it would look bad. So it was policy that workers were not allowed to fraternize with guests and were strictly prohibited from being in their rooms.

One day there were some new staff members who were busboys and waiters from Italy, Germany and other European Countries on the beach, and I approached them and informed them that they should not be there mingling with the guests of the hotel, that they should go to the public beach next door. They were sitting and talking with four young ladies who were guests at the hotel, and absolutely paid me no mind, as if I had not said anything to them. I informed them again of the policy, and that they should leave but they did not. I informed the hotel manager as it was part of my job duties. Shortly after speaking with the staff members, one of the guests who was sitting with the staff came to tell me that she had seen a few Man-of-Wars in the water and that the ladies wanted to go swimming. I went into the water, and since there were only a few, picked them up with my bare hands, a technique that I had mastered over the years which avoided me from being stung by the tentacles, brought them back to shore, and buried them in the sand. I then explained to the swimmers that they had a half hour for swimming as the current was moving slowly, and it would be at least that amount of time before any more Man-of-Wars floated by.

Just as I had predicted to the guest about the time that the Man-of-Wars would come floating by based on the current, another one of the young ladies came running up to me to tell me that she had seen another Man-of-War. I immediately went to get the Man-of-War, but on my way I noticed that one of the newer staff members that I told to not congregate with the ladies was going towards the Man-of-War, so I shouted out to him "*Get away from that!*" and he looked at me, as I repeated myself "*Get away from that!*". He totally ignored me and kept swimming toward the Man-of-War. Immediately after he gripped the Man-of-War, it stung him so hard that I actually saw his knees come out of the water in a stand-up position, and he hollered loudly in pain. Being angry with him for not listening to me, I shouted out to him to come to shore, keep swimming in. When he finally came to shore, he sat and was trembling with tentacles all over his body, including his face. I tended to him by removing the tentacles with a towel and vinegar, and I then told him about the painful process that he would be going through.

Shortly after I had returned to my station, another guest came up to me to tell me that they had seen another Man-of-War, so I left my station and went into the water and gripped the Man-of-War and brought him to shore and buried him. On my way back to my station, the young man who had been stung and it was visibly clear that he was still in a lot of pain, and was still trembling and shaking, called to me and asked me "*How come you don't get stung?"* and still angry with him for not listening to my warning, I replied, *"Didn't they tell you that Man-of-Wars don't sting Black people?"* He looked at me as if to say *"Well, how does the Man-of-War know the difference between a Black or White person?"* Three minutes later, the hotel manager came up to me and asked me, *"Where are the staff members?"* and I pointed him to them and he then approached them, and they all left the beach immediately. Those staff members were given probation and were told if they were ever caught on the premises with the guests again they would be fired.

CHAPTER SIXTEEN
The Undercurrent

There was one particular time while working at Elbow Beach, a guest came to say that he was having a birthday and wanted to have about one hundred and fifteen people come off the cruise ship to the beach here. He informed me that he was Jewish, but that made no difference to me as I gave service to all guests no matter what religion or nationality, that was the way I handled people, with respect. He wanted to pay for all one hundred and fifteen chairs and umbrellas for his guests. As the Head Beach Attendant, I explained I can give him the chairs and about half the umbrellas and would set them up in a way that was suitable. He paid me, and working by myself, I set the umbrellas between two chairs each. He explained about sixty to seventy guests will come before noon, and the other half will come about two o'clock.

The first group arrived, and they were all enjoying themselves and the Jewish man got up to go swimming himself. Well, he got caught in the undercurrent. The undercurrent is a type of current which runs below the surface of the water in the opposite direction of the surface water. It can be very strong at times, which if you are swimming and get caught up in one, the first thing people do (which is what they should not do) is panic. If you are caught in an undercurrent, you should swim across or parallel to the shore, not headed immediately towards the shore. All of his friends were on the edge of the beach, screaming for a lifeguard. I left my station and went down to where he was, and I could see him struggling and calling for help, but he was not drowning. I was trying to coach him how to get out of this situation by coming towards me, explaining to him that he needs to swim parallel to the shore towards me, and I was motioning to him where he should go. As he was still yelling for help, not following my directions, his wife, in a panic, slapped me hard on the back telling me to go get him.

Since the man was not listening to my directions, I swam closer to him in the water to help direct him, still being mindful that oftentimes when people are in a panic, they may unintentionally grab on to me and cause me to be compromised when I am trying to save them. Also, it is worth noting that he was able to breathe and yell, which means he was not drowning. When I was about five feet from him, he was still flapping his arms, and I went a little too close to him, and he grabbed my right arm with both his hands in a death grip as he was heavier than I was, making it difficult to pull him in. Based on my training and skills, in order to get him to calm down, I had to shift my body to get behind him, and I took my hand and put it over his nose and mouth and squeezed his nose. This immediately made him let go and he took his hands off me which allowed me to put my hand under his chin. He floated to the top of the water like a balloon, and it was at this point I was able to paddle him into the shore. Once we got to the point where I was waist high where I could stand, I tried to get him to put his feet down, but for some reason, his body kept afloat on top of the water like a balloon. So I had to lift him up in a standing position and drop him so his feet could touch the bottom of the ocean. It was at this point, where his knees were out of the water, he ran out of my arms, immediately to his lounge chair, not a word said to me. One or two people thanked me, and I just went back to my normal work as it seemed as if no medical attention was needed.

At about two o'clock, the other thirty-forty of his guests came to the beach, looking for the birthday guy. I pointed out to them where he was and they called out his name, and he jumped out of his chair when the guest called him saying, "*Oh man, you should have been here, you should have been here. You missed my show!*" He was boasting about flailing in the water and making a big production really loud on the beach, saying he was pretending to drown and really acting up. It was at this point a frequent female guest to the hotel who witnessed the whole incident got out of her chair and walked over to the gentleman and gave him one slap across his face. You could hear that sound all across the whole beach. She hollered at him, "*You should be ashamed of yourself, you were hollering and putting on a show and this man risked his life to save you, and you were pretending! You should be ashamed.*"

Well, after that, the man was really quiet, and the rest of the guests still enjoyed themselves at the beach. When it was time to leave, as folks were departing at different times to make it back to the cruise ship, there were only about four people left, the Jewish man, his wife, and two of his friends. As I was moving about the beach, collecting the one hundred and fifteen chairs and umbrellas, I noticed he was avoiding my eyes and was avoiding going past me, which you had to do to exit the beach. I tested this thought as I moved away from my post to collect some more umbrellas, and they quickly ran off. I have a feeling they were embarrassed for his actions, but after all of that, he never even tipped me or thanked me.

I haven't given many stories of the numerous rescues while being a lifeguard, but there were many; of people either caught in the undercurrent, encountering man-of wars, etc. At any given time, the circumstances can change very quickly. If you ask how many people do you think I have pulled from the water, it could be as high as eighteen persons a year, another year it could be between ten to twelve, and some days, thankfully it is none. I want you to know I never lost not one person in my forty-one years.

CHAPTER SEVENTEEN
Miss Jane

◦

My experience as a lifeguard and Superintendent at the Elbow Beach Hotel for over forty years (from 1956 to 1997) showed me some of the many faces of prejudice and disrespect in so many different ways. One experience that stands out to me, is of a middle aged White woman, who we will call Miss Jane. Miss Jane was a great friend of Mickey Caines, the manager of the beach facilities. As a courtesy to her, he had arranged with me that any time Miss Jane came to the beach that I would give her a free towel and the use of the facilities, a task which I had done for the past three years.

On many occasions, I would go into the Phoenix Store where Miss Jane worked and whenever I saw her, I would always speak. As a Bermudian, it is rude to not speak when you are greeted or entering a space with people already there. Miss Jane never acknowledged me, and this went on for a very long time. I finally got tired of it, because I knew that she knew who I was, since I was the one providing her a towel and the use of the facilities weekly. The next time Miss Jane came to the beach I said to her *"I have known you for three years, and every time you come to the beach I take care of you by giving you a free towel, locker and the use of the facilities, but whenever I come into the Phoenix and I speak to you, you pretend that you don't even know me, so as of today, I will not be giving you any special treatment."*

Much to my surprise, she broke down and cried and she then went up to the upper verandah and sat there until Mickey came to her. He then brought Miss Jane back down to see me, and I told him that I was not going to give her any towels or anything because whenever I saw her in public she acted as if she did not know me. I did not know what to expect, but Mickey then told her that when he was not there I am in charge and she has to respect me for doing my job. He further stated Mr. Bean has always been polite to you. It was at that point she apologized for her behaviour and wouldn't you know from that day on whenever I went into Town and the Phoenix Store, she would make it a point to come up to me from nowhere and say "*Good morning Renee*" and I would respond "*Good Morning Miss Jane.*"

CHAPTER EIGHTEEN
Who Respects Who?
❦

Sunday's was always a busy time at the Elbow Beach with many guests and locals coming there for "Sunday Brunch". Sunday brunch at the time, was where restaurants have a buffet style brunch with all assortment of foods, complete with traditional Bermuda breakfast of Codfish & Potatoes and other things. The hotel always offered a "special pass" for outside guests who wished to use the beach facilities that day as this was part of the package with the Sunday Brunch, they had to ask for it.

One particular Sunday, a gentleman with a party of eighteen approached me saying that they had just had brunch at the hotel, and they were entitled to use the beach facilities. Yes, I agreed with him and said to him "*May I have your pass,*" and he replied "*What pass?*" I responded, "*You need a pass for yourself and guests so that I can register you to use the facilities here.*" He arrogantly answered me back by saying "*I don't have one.*" I asked him if he or one of his guests could go back to the hotel and get one, and he said, "*No, we are not going to get one,*" and then he bullied himself through by pushing past me.

Shortly after he bullied pass me, I was able to stop the rest of the group from getting by. He was about thirty yards onto the beach when he looked back and saw his wife and the rest of the party to the top of the steps stopped by me. He shouted out to her "*Come on down honey,*" and she replied by saying "*He's not going to let us through.*" Well, he came back to the entrance and said "*Excuse me*" to move past myself, going back up the steps. I let him pass me going towards the party, and he again shouted out for the party to come down with him on the beach. As the party neared the entrance where I was, he then forcibly shoved me back with his right arm to open space for his party to come through. At this point, I was totally shocked, embarrassed, humiliated, and very disrespected at the way he had literally shoved me to get past.

I jumped up because he was about six-feet tall, and fired my right hand towards him and it landed on his left jaw. He was knocked unconscious in one blow and it took a few minutes for him to come to. The whole party was frightened at the interaction and they all screamed when they realized that he was unconscious.

After the incident, the party went back to the hotel to make a complaint, and shortly thereafter returned back to the beach with the pass. I then gladly gave them the use of the beach facilities with the proper pass. Early the next morning, the manager called me and asked me to come up to the office immediately. With his tone and the urgency in his voice, I knew that it had to do with what had happened at the beach with that party the day before.

When I arrived at the manager's office, before I could sit down, he announced that I could be suspended for a couple of weeks or lose my job because of that interaction. I replied, "*Where's my Shop Stewart?*" who is the Union representative for the workers. He immediately picked up the telephone and called for the Shop Steward. Once the Shop Stewart arrived, the manager started to read the "Letter of Complaint", which was filed by the group. It read:

> *"I had a party of eighteen here for Sunday brunch and then we went to the beach afterwards, where we met Rene Bean who asked us for*

> *a pass. I told him that I didn't have one and he asked if one of us could go back up and get one. I told him that I was not going back to get a pass and I then pushed Rene aside to let my wife and party through and he responded by hitting me."*

After hearing the complaint, the Shop Stewart told the manager that I could not be suspended, because the complainant was the aggressor by putting his hands on me first and pushing me aside. On that note, I was sent immediately back to the job.

I had realized that this particular manager who had called me in his office to deal with the complaint did not like me very much after that. For about two weeks, he approached me with a nasty attitude and jeered at me about how the complainant was going to take me to court. I said to him *"Good, because I am going to take him to Immigration."* The next day the manager came down to the beach trying to be all humble and polite, even asking me how my day was. I responded back to him *"Just as good as every other day!"* The manager then went on to explain how the gentleman had changed his mind about the decision of taking me to Court. My thoughts behind that was that the manager knew I was serious about going to Immigration as one or two of his friends had been already deported from

Lifeguard on duty

Bermuda because I had gone to Immigration, due to their total disrespect of me, and lack of following the policies in place - similar behavior of this gentleman.

CHAPTER NINETEEN
The Red-Haired Man and His New Position

A group of about fifteen young guest workers came to the beach one day after having brunch. Guest workers are foreigners who come to the island for job opportunities and typically had contracts for about a year or so. Renewal of their permission to work and stay in Bermuda depended on a number of things, one of them being a good citizen, or having good behavior. As hotel policy for guests dictates the use of beach facilities, I asked them for their pass because they are assigned to a special area from the regular guest staying at the hotel. While asking for their pass, one red-headed guy who was clearly intoxicated swore at me and called me a "***F...g Black Nigga***". I said to him, "I *need the pass, because I cannot let you on the beach without it.*" He reacted by attempting to throw a punch at me, but I stepped aside while his friends held him back. They then left by pulling him to the west end of the beach - the public area.

At the end of my shift I went to play tennis at the courts, which was next to the car park and I noticed a red car and a black car still parked there. While playing tennis, I was watching to see when the group of guest workers returned to their cars, so that I could see which car the "red-headed guy" got in. When I saw him enter the red car, I took the number of that car. The next day, I did some research and had a friend inform me of the name and address of the driver of the red car. I then went to the address and I saw the driver of the red car who I recognized as one of the fellow that was with the group. I asked him if he remembered me and he replied, "*Yes, I do,*" and that I worked at Elbow Beach. I then replied to him, "*I* don't want to include you in this, but I would like for you to give me the name of the red-haired guy who cussed me and tried to attack me." He replied "*No, I can't give it to you.*" I then said, "Look, *I really don't want to include you, I just want the red-haired guy's name.*" and he replied "*No.*" for the second time. I then said to him "*Well, since you don't want to give me his name, you will be included in my complaint along with the red-head.*"

The following week, the beach police patrol showed up, and I approached them to explain what had happened. I also gave them the name and the car number of the driver of the red car, and also told them about the red-headed guy who had cussed me, and called me a slew of names including trying to throw a punch at me. Surprisingly, early the next Monday morning, I received a phone call from the police, asking me to come to the police station. When I arrived, a policeman took me aside and explained to me that they had these two guys in a back cell. They then asked me to identify them and when I went in and saw them, much to my surprise, it was the same two guys. They were in suits which were dirty and wrinkled. I realized that they had to have been arrested on the prior Friday night, so that meant that they had spent the whole weekend in jail.

The policeman then asked me if they were the two guys that were involved in the incident at the Elbow Beach and I replied "*Yes,*" and at that time I told the two guys that I would like a written apology, but I never did receive one. The policeman then took me in a separate room and said to me "*We know that you are a hard worker and that you like your job, and you will only lose time and money if you take these guys to court.*" He further explained how the case is going to be two against one, eventually the whole bunch of friends would most likely back him and it would only be me, and I would have difficulty in winning because they have friends that would back the guys up whatever story was told. After the policeman made it clear that I would not win my case, he recommended that since I have their names now I should take it to Immigration.

Upon the policeman's advice I scurried off to Immigration to report the incident against these guys. When the Immigration Officer pulled the records for the individuals, they found that the first guys' work permit would expire in two months and should he apply for a new permit, his application would come up for review as a result of this incident. They also noticed that the red-haired guy had recently applied for a new job and had been offered the position, but was waiting for Immigration approval; but after hearing my complaint the officer informed me they would have to review his application again.

Two weeks had passed after I visited the guys in jail, and lo and behold on one of my busiest days at the beach, with hundreds of guests lined up to enter the beach, I looked up and saw the red-haired guy standing on the side of the line. He waited until the crowds were all on the beach and he approached me by saying "*Rene, we have been friends since...,*" and he continued by showing me a letter which his lawyer had written and wanted me to sign. During this time, he was brawling loudly and at the same time calling England more names than what he had called me, because he did not want to go back to England, and he definitely did not want to leave Bermuda. I told him that I am not signing any letter and, even if I did

Immigration, were not going to change their minds. They were all mad at me, based on the incident, but at the same time the friends knew not to challenge me because I had some power in just doing my job. Not too long after I refused to sign the red-head's letter, the group showed up at Elbow Beach with a large trunk in the car, as this was their "farewell drink" to celebrate their friend's return to England.

CHAPTER TWENTY
The Red-Haired Lady and Her New Volkswagen

Elbow Beach was quite a popular place for the foreign guest workers to get together and enjoy their day off, and oftentimes to come and show their visiting guests off. A "guest worker" were considered folks who were brought into Bermuda who were permitted to work for different companies. Guest workers were typically White. Over the years, one of the things that I recognized about the guest workers was that after being on the island for a while and getting their feet on the ground, they seem to have a problem with respecting any Black Bermudian who was in any capacity as Superintendent or manager. No matter how hospitable the Bermudian was to them they seemed to show total disrespect, especially when they had their visiting family and friends with them.

One day a group of foreign workers came to the beach with friends and family who were visiting them from overseas. As soon as they arrived, they just went and took beach chairs, umbrellas and used the shower facilities. Whenever any guests come to the beach, there are signs stating that they have to pay to use these facilities. When I approached a red haired young lady who frequently came to the beach and told her that they have to pay for the use of the facilities, a lady who was with her said, "*Don't pay attention to that uneducated fool.*" The red-haired lady responded by saying, "*I never do.*" I then responded back to the lady who had called me an uneducated fool by saying to her, "*I will show you what an uneducated fool can do!*"

When the lady called me an uneducated fool, and the red-haired guest worker responded the way she did, I had never felt so humiliated and embarrassed in my life, because as they made their comments I was serving two repeat guests of the hotel. The gentleman said to me, "*Why are they being so rude to you, because you are such a nice person and always treat others with respect, I have never seen you disrespect anyone!*" I replied, "*Don't worry, I'm taking this to another level. I will be checking with her boss, because I know the hotel where she is employed.*"

To set my plan in motion, I needed a full rainy day, because it would give me the opportunity to carry out my plan, as I would not be needed on the job. One week later, I was finally blessed with a full day of rain and was able to visit the resort where the red-haired lady worked. I went there to talk with her boss, who was a White Bermudian. When we met, I told him of the incident and asked if he would give me her name. He refused to give it to me and he told me that I should report the incident to Mickey Caines as he was my boss and let him deal with it. I told him, "*I don't want him to deal with it, because he would not deal with it the way that I would.*" A few minutes after the manager and I departed, I saw a young Bermudian lady, who was introduced to me earlier by the Bellman, and I spoke with her asking if she knew the name of a red-haired lady, and she eagerly gave me her name and told me the department where she worked.

After leaving the hotel, I jumped on my bike and in the pouring rain I rode straight into Hamilton to go to the Immigration Department. When I met with the Immigration Officer, and related the incident which had occurred with the red-haired lady and her visiting guest, I then explained to

him that I had worked at the Elbow Beach for over thirty years at that point, and in
all of my affairs with people, I treat everyone with respect. I explained that day I took the abuse, because I never dealt with racial issues- Black and White issues in front of my other guests. The Officer took the information from me, and he then pulled her file, and when he showed me her picture, I jumped saying " *Yes, Yes, that's her!*"

Shortly after my visit with Immigration, the Executive Manager of Elbow Beach called me to his office, and when I arrived, he showed me a slew of letters and phone calls he had received from the manager of the resort where the red-haired lady worked. There were also many letters from her friends, which were all saying how nice of a person she was, so the manager asked me " *What is this all about?*". I said to him that she and her friends had come down to the beach, took use of the facilities and towels without paying. When I politely informed her that she needed to pay for the use of the facilities, one of her guests said, "*Don't listen to that uneducated fool*" and she responded with," I *never do!*", in front of my other guests. I further explained at that time I did not want to deal with the obvious disrespect and racially motivated dismissal of my position in front of other guests, so I reported it to Immigration. After hearing what I had to say, the manager said, "*Rene, all that I have heard is second-hand,*" and at that point he ripped the letters to shreds, threw them all in the trash and said, "*Rene, you are my best worker, go back to work.*"

While visiting with Immigration, I was made to understand that the red-haired lady's contract was set to expire the end of that particular month, and after a while I learned that just before this incident, she had bought herself a brand new Volkswagen, because she was looking forward to a long stay in Bermuda, but as a result of my complaint within that time she was deported from the island. Ironically, after the incidents with the red-haired guy and the red-haired lady, the rest of the foreign workers seemed to take a liking to me, as they all started to treat me with respect by addressing me as, "*Sir*" or saying "*Good Day Rene.*"

CHAPTER TWENTY-ONE
The Bermuda Triangle Mysteries

I have seen many documentaries, written reports, and other theories from around the world about the Bermuda Triangle, but I have never heard any experiences from Bermudians, who I feel have seen unexplainable and strange things out in the ocean firsthand. The Bermuda Triangle is a part of the Atlantic Ocean between Bermuda, Florida, and Puerto Rico. A number of aircrafts and ships have disappeared under what was believed to be mysterious circumstances. You never heard of the Florida triangle, or Puerto Rico triangle, and the mysterious occurrences could be closer to those countries, however it is blamed on Bermuda. I must say, I myself believe that I have seen a few things that were quite unexplainable.

My first experience that I had with the Bermuda Triangle Mysteries, was as I was driving past Church Bay, and I saw a gentleman who I knew looking at the ocean in a trance-like state, so I immediately pulled over to see what he was looking at. To my surprise, I saw a sheet of snow White water about sixteen feet in circumference bubbling about a foot or so higher than water level. I stood there and this motion went on for about a half hour from the time I had arrived. I believe that both the gentleman and I were in such shock that we just left without saying a word to each other, and I never told anyone about what I had seen, as they would not have believed me, or thought to themselves that I was a bit crazy.

It was about a month later that I was watching a documentary on television where a scientist was explaining his theory on how ships disappear. He demonstrated by having a model ship in a large tub-like structure, and he opened an air vial which was at the bottom of the tub. When the vial was opened, air bubbles formed and were rising from the bottom of the tub. This action caused the model ship to sink, and lo and behold, I realized that this was the same reaction of what I had seen at Church Bay. The ship actually sank to the bottom of the tub and when he closed the vial, the ship resurfaced.

Another experience that I had was with my sister Gilda and her husband, Jimmy Mello, and six of their friends who were visiting from the U.S. My sister and her husband had asked if I would take their friends for a BBQ Cruise on my boat and that they would pay for the fuel. The day was calm and sunny and there was no wind or anything at all. We arrived on the south side of Port's Island which was a popular camping island for Bermudians and we tied up to a mooring that was already there. I then shut down the engine and started to set up the BBQ. The water was as smooth as glass, when all of a sudden, the boat made a 360-degree slow turn, picking up pace, and this happened twice. There was no wind blowing to turn the boat, and no bad weather in the area over us. We all just stood there in total disbelief, because we could not understand why it was turning in a circle for about two minutes, and without hesitation, I told my brother-in-law to untie the rope up front and I started the engine and we got out of there as fast as we could without anyone saying a word, as it was strange and frightening and we were all dumbfounded. I drove the boat straight back to Riddle's Bay wharf, where we set up the BBQ on dry land.

I believe other mysteries relating to activity caused by the Bermuda Triangle happened October 31, 1981 on a very busy Saturday morning while working at Elbow Beach as a lifeguard. There were about seven hundred chairs and umbrellas set-up, and quite a number of people laying on the beach. At around ten thirty, to the far East, I saw a bright light shining on the water which was coming from the reflection of the sun and this light really caught my attention. The more I looked at it, the more I realized that something strange was happening in the ocean. This strange thing seemed to grow larger and it appeared as if it was propelled by a huge propeller as water was being churned with angry motion, moving quite rapidly westward. I could see that a storm was coming, so I immediately ordered all the umbrellas to be pulled own and then ordered the guest to leave the beach, but because they could not see what I could see, there was some resistance from the guests, but upon hearing the urgency in my voice, they all went off to the clubhouse none too pleased.

    I realize that this was no ordinary storm, because as I watched from my office on the beach, I could not believe what I was seeing! The ocean itself was like a sheet of glass, but what I saw was the formation of what appeared to be a waterspout, but with a much larger body. As this body of water rose up to between two to three hundred feet, it then curled over and landed about four hundred feet forward, dispersing tons of water and then it would pick up again and toss water another four hundred feet, with the ocean becoming very rough. Each time it landed, you could hear a loud bang which sounded like the roar of thunder. This continued all the way to the West, until it disappeared from my sight. Although the storm never approached land, each time the waves landed in the ocean, they were so powerful they threw big drops of water on the beach as if they were rain drops, but these drops were as large as human footprints.

Later that evening I learned that four of my friends; Johnny Riley, Kenny Thompson, Eugene Pearman and Harry Arorash; who were all family men and good sportsmen, well known to the public, were out fishing during the time of this supernatural storm and were lost at sea, their bodies were never found. I believe that the strange phenomena that I witnessed would have crushed them to death instantly and I truly believe that they did not suffer.

CHAPTER TWENTY-TWO
Waterspouts and Tornadoes

The devastation of hurricanes is something that has long lasting effects on many parts of the island. Over the years, I have seen many storms, tornadoes, hurricanes and waterspouts that have come across this Island of Bermuda. When I was a young boy of twelve, my friends and I would go to the Southlands Estate, which was located on South Shore Road in Warwick, and had been abandoned for many years. There were two large banyan trees which looked like two large mushrooms that had many vines hanging from them, and we would swing on them and pretend that we were Tarzan.

After leaving there we would wander across the road where we would visit what we thought were old bomb shelters and we called them "Bulldozers." These bomb shelters were located on the cliffs and we would enter them by making loud noises so that we could hear the sound echo back to us which was quite noisy. The Americans located here in Bermuda at the time would use this area for target practice by shooting at a plane which flew by the area and the plane had orange or yellow targets towing about a thousand yards behind.

On this particular day, we were getting ready to go home when we noticed a waterspout in the ocean that seemed to be coming towards us, so we ran back into the Bulldozer to hide, and we chose a smaller one to be protected as we can hide behind a wall. As we were waiting, we heard a funny noise from the waterspout as it hit the cliff. Our ears became clogged and we could not hear much after that. It lasted only a few minutes, and while it was happening, we had difficulty breathing as it passed us. Once the waterspout hits the ground, it becomes a tornado. Once the waterspout had passed us, we noticed that the air had been sucked out as if it had been vacuumed right out, and we had difficulty breathing. Once we got outside there was a feeling in the air that we could not explain.

When we left the area, we were heading for home at Spring Hill. We had to cross the Edness Estate, which is on the west side of Billy Goat Hill. As we were crossing the estate we noticed a pathway of fallen cedar trees and branches. We could see one house that was completely flattened, and recognized the house as being owned by Mr. Prime, who was a West-Indian living in Bermuda, a very good tailor who did work for the whole neighborhood. After seeing this, we then realized that the waterspout that we had seen earlier had turned into a tornado! We saw some tragic sights on our way home as the tornado had lifted a German Shepard dog and his kennel, which was in the backyard of my neighbor's home, and it tossed it over an electrical wire, leaving the dog hanging on one side and the kennel on the other by his chain. This had electrocuted him.

When I arrived home, I could not believe what I saw. The tornado had dropped a very large tree trunk in my yard which had put a large indent in the house, which was built of limestone. When I went in and told my family what had happened, they could not believe it, as they were all at home. No one had heard anything, and it was more surprising to them when they all went outside and saw the large tree trunk and the size of the indent in the house. It took three strong men to remove that cedar trunk from our house, and thankfully everyone was alright.

Bermuda blue waters

CHAPTER TWENTY-THREE
Shark Attack

In my youth, my friends and I used to go swimming at the Atlantic Beach Club, which was located on the South Shore Road in Warwick. Quite often while swimming there, we would see three to four-foot sharks swimming around us, but no one was ever attacked. In those days, everyone went fishing, because that was one way of getting food for the family, and it was a well-known fact that on a full moon night there would be several sharks in the area. This one particular night I caught four sharks that were four feet long. During my time as a life-guard at Elbow Beach, I used to take the guests from the hotel snorkeling along the reefs and they would explore the beautiful coral formations and colorful fish.

In the 1960's Bermuda brought in many expatriate workers from overseas to do work in the hotels and restaurant industry, to do such jobs as waiters, busboys and bartenders. On the 24th May 1960, there was a shark attack in Bermuda at the west end of Elbow Beach. On the day of the shark attack, there was a group of expatriates who had just come to Bermuda to work at the hotel, and on their first visit to the beach, they were so excited to see such beautiful water they just took off into the water and snorkeled out to the reefs. None of them had any experience in swimming around coral reefs and several of them got cut up and bruised, which meant on their way back to shore, they left a trail of blood in the water. About fifteen minutes after coming into shore, one of the workers decided to go back in the water to wash the sand and blood off his body and while standing waist high, a ten-foot shark came up to him attacking his legs as the shark had caught a scent of blood. Fortunately, the worker managed to push the shark away with just a graze on his knee and fingers. He was also able to get out of the water quickly as the shark kept circling that area. One of the beach attendants ran to the hotel to get a piece of meat and in the meantime, myself and the other attendant put together a fishing line with a large hook. There was a young man in a punt nearby who drove a spear right through the shark before it could take the line bait and the shark lost its sense and ended up on the beach flipping and flopping until it died.

Another near shark attack happened in the summer of 1998 and at this time I had left the hotel working as a lifeguard, as the hotel had made me redundant after working there for over forty years. After making my job redundant and with a good severance package, I was able to purchase my own taxi and began driving taxi as my next career move. One day in the summer of 1998, while driving tourists from Dockyard to Horseshoe Bay, I stopped off at the lay-by above Horseshoe Bay to allow the tourists to see the beach, and to take pictures. I immediately noticed that the people on the beach were lined up on the water's edge in knee deep water, staring off into the water, and I instantly knew that there was a shark about. Within a few seconds a very large shark swam into view and the shark travelled the full length of the beach, so I jumped into my taxi and raced down to the beach.

When I got on there, I approached about seven life-guards, and asked if one of them could go to the next beach to get the people out of the water, because that shark is hungry, but they seemed reluctant to go, and because it seemed they did not want to take any orders from a stranger. Eventually, one did go and at that time I went to the highest point of

Horseshoe Bay, where I had a full view of the shark and could see it circling at a great speed from one end of the beach to the other. After realizing that there was only one shark, I could hear the people screaming that there were five or six sharks! The reason why they were saying that it was more than one shark was because each time the shark re-surfaced to turn around at the end of the beach, the dorsal fin was always showing, and every time it appeared at the opposite end of the beach, they would count it as another shark.

The shark then swam to the middle of the beach facing the people with its dorsal fin out of the water for about twenty seconds, and it seemed to me that it was contemplating whether or not it would attack. The shark then suddenly took off, charging the people who were standing knee high in the water, with great speed, and beaching itself right up on the beach, and raising its head with its mouth wide open as if looking for its next meal. Still standing high on the cliff, it was a chaotic sight to see people running helter skelter, leaving the beach screaming, falling down, stumbling over themselves just to get as far away from the shark as possible. After about fifteen seconds of being beached on the sand, a wave came in and touched the shark under its tail and it wiggled a bit and was able to turn its body towards the ocean, and on the third wave it swam away.

After watching the chaotic state and confusion going on, I left the top of the cliff and was about to leave the beach when a reporter, whom I knew, came directly to me to ask questions, as he knew that I was a lifeguard and he wanted to see what information I had about the shark. While I was explaining to the reporter that the shark was ten feet long and that there was

only one shark, before I could finish, a woman who was standing nearby, rudely and
abruptly cut into my conversation by saying *"Don't pay attention to him, because they say it was five or six sharks!"* I was so stunned to hear her say *"they say,"* meaning she did not see the shark herself. She then went on to say who she was and that she was the manager of the Bermuda Underwater Exploration Institute (BUEI) and she then repeated that *"they"* said there were five or six sharks.

    At this point I knew she had not seen anything herself and was just going on what *"they"* said. I was feeling insulted and hurt due to the fact that first, I actually witnessed the shark with my own eyes, second, as a former lifeguard of nearly forty years, I could properly identify the size and number of sharks present, third, the reporter continued listening to her hearsay, not on what I witnessed. I witnessed the whole event and movement of the shark, so I just walked away. Later that evening I was happy to see a video which the broadcasting studio had borrowed from a tourist, which showed everything that I had witnessed, showing only one large shark when it was beached. My only hope was that the Manager from BUEI saw that clip as well!

CHAPTER TWENTY-FOUR
Mike and His Red Dinghy

For a number of years, Mike often drove his red dinghy up and down the South Shore, stopping off at the beaches. A dinghy is the name of a small boat, and Mike was a Portuguese Bermudian, very tall, who had represented Bermuda in the Pan Am games in high jumping at one point. As the lifeguard and beach attendant at Elbow Beach Hotel, we had become friends over the years, he even nicknamed me "Coco". This particular day around two-thirty in the afternoon I noticed Mike's red dinghy off the shore at Elbow Beach and it was not moving- therefore I thought he was fishing.

It was a very busy day with a continuous stream of tourists and more than five hundred chairs and umbrellas scattered along the beach waiting to be packed away, and I had paid no attention to the dinghy throughout the day. By the time I was ready to leave it was about eight-thirty p.m., and daylight was slowly fading as I entered the hotel entrance to clock out. When I entered the hotel, I was met by two tourists who told me that a man had fallen out of his boat and could not get back in. When I looked out at the shore, I could see a dinghy tilting to the side and I immediately knew it was Mike. On my way to the beach I knew that I had to swim, because someone had cut a hole in my rubber rescue boat that I noticed earlier on. My only fear of swimming this day was being stung in the face by a Man-of-War, because several guests had been stung that same day, and here it was night and I could not see them in the dark.

The last of the sunset was my guiding light as I jumped into the water, and I immediately was plagued with thoughts of the newly released

"Jaws" movie as I swam towards the reefs. I swam with my eyes open. By the time I reached the reefs it was dark and I truly regretted watching "Jaws" as every shadow beneath me looked like a shark. The dark spots under me were actually rocks or reefs deep down. Struggling to keep my focus on getting to Mike, I stood on the reef to survey the remaining distance beyond the reefs and the boat, which was over a hundred yards and much deeper water of approximately eighty to one hundred feet. I jumped back into the water heading towards the barely visible dinghy, and with every stroke my heart was pounding faster and faster and the entire time that I was swimming, only thinking about the possibility of sharks and Man-of-Wars! I did not want to swim with my head underwater doing a technique called the American Crawl, again for fear of getting stung in my face by a Man-of-War, so I had to swim with my head above water which caused me to use up a lot of energy, also to keep my eyes on the boat because of the darkness and the currents.

With every stroke, I was also listening out to hear if I heard Mike holler out as the thought of a shark attacking him came to mind and if that was the case, I would have swam back to shore, but the only sound that I heard were my arms slapping against the water. When I finally reached the dinghy, I grabbed it and hauled myself up as fast as I could, relieved that I was out of the water! In my hurry to get into the boat, I knocked over a bottle of rum, which explained Mike's situation, and I immediately picked up the bottle and dumped the rest of the rum in the ocean. When he felt the boat move, Mike called out, "*Who is it? Coco is that you?*" I replied, "*Yes!*" and I gripped his wrist as he gripped mine. Holding onto the dinghy with my other hand, I gave one big pull, and Mike, who was close to six feet and weighed over two-hundred pounds, slid right in on the floor of the dinghy.

As he lay on the floor trembling and his skin all wrinkled from being in the water, he said it was over six hours of him being there. He cried aloud repeatedly saying that he thought that he was going to be there all night. When he finally caught himself, he thanked me, got up, started his engine and took me ashore, and off he went back out into the dark ocean with no lights heading towards Devonshire Bay. Knowing that Mike was sober at that point, I still worried all night whether he had made it to his destination. The next day, I listened for the missing person news report and even checked the newspaper; however, it was not until around four p.m. that I felt a sigh of relief, as I watched Mike in his red dinghy as he passed by the beach.

CHAPTER TWENTY-FIVE
A Lifeguard's Duty-
The Untold Story of a Heroic Rescue

On a warm summer day while I was serving as a lifeguard at Elbow Beach, my attention was gained by a group of people to the east of the beach, on the Stonington Beach property, screaming for help for a lifeguard. I immediately ran to the frantic individuals who told me that there were four Portuguese or Caucasian Bermudian boys out in the water. At this time, a hurricane was several hundred miles off Bermuda, causing huge rolling swells along the south shore coastline. Along with the swells there was lots of undercurrent. The undercurrent is a strong tide that pushes swimmers out to sea. The swells and tides were so high that the water had consumed half the beach. I looked out on the water at the area where they were pointing, but could not see anyone.

I am a strong and experienced swimmer, and I made two attempts to get past the waves, but each time they pushed me right back. On the third attempt, I dove under the waves and swam underwater until I was beyond the crashing waves and surf. As I resurfaced, I sighted one of the boys and he pointed to the location of the other three boys. The boy who I first sighted managed to make it safely to shore. The other three were further out, with the current pushing them even further. Two of the boys were holding the third boy whose swimming abilities were limited. When I got within eighty feet of the boys, I saw one of them holding the third boy, let go of him and began swimming towards shore. He passed by me at about sixty feet and said that he was exhausted and could not hold on any longer.

When I was about forty feet from the final two, the last boy holding onto his friend could no longer hold on and he let go and headed for shore. As the boy let go of his friend, the non-swimming friend disappeared under the surging swells of the ocean.

At this point, my lifeguard training kicked in. I focused on the spot where he disappeared, with about thirty feet to go I raced to the location. Due to the white surging water, visibility underwater was nil. The water was milky white. Fortunately, when I got nearer to the location, I went underwater for about fifteen feet doing the breaststroke, and as my arms made the wide sweeping motion, I touched him with my left hand, still unable to see, I turned and gripped him and brought him to the surface, his body limp. There was no indication of life, so I applied pressure to his stomach and as I applied pressure, he vomited a lot of water. I repeated this action several times with him vomiting the salt water each time. Even though he had brought up, there was still no indication of life. His body was so limp, I was certain that he was dead, but while carrying him to shore I made certain to keep his head above water.

After twenty minutes, I glanced towards shore and I was surprised to see an old man by the name of Skinner behind me. Thinking that he would be of some help, Mr. Skinner unexpectedly dived underwater, gripped the boy's feet and brought them to the surface. This caused the young man and myself to go under water. As I resurfaced, I shouted to Mr. Skinner to let the boy's feet go and to go and get help from ashore. My shouting at Mr. Skinner caused me to swallow seawater and I choked and choked. As I tried to clear my throat, my eyes were watering and I had difficulty breathing and it took me about ten minutes before I could catch myself. All I could see were big walls of water and sky, it seemed as if I was in a gutter.

The currents were so strong that I could not make any headway towards shore. While treading water, I began to fear for my own life. Each time I was carried to the pinnacle of a wave, I could see what seemed to me as hundreds of people on the shoreline. I could also see the ambulance crew and many police. My expectations were high. I felt for certain that someone would be coming to help, but it never happened. No one else came into the water to help. My hands were hurting from shifting the boy from arm to arm while continually treading water. By this time, the waves had consumed all of Stonington Beach and they were crashing against the bank and the onlookers were no longer watching on the beach, but instead had moved up to the bank. While struggling to head west away from the rocky reefs, I thought about letting him go, but just could not. I did not know whether I could not let him go because of my cramped fingers being locked on him, or because of my lifeguard oath.

It seemed like two hours had passed as I treaded water waiting for help. I began to wonder if I ran the two-hundred yards too fast, or had I used too much energy on my attempts to get through the waves, or had I used too much speed during that last ten yards when diving for him? I put demand on the Lord through prayer to get us in. After a few moments after my prayer, two large waves seemed to push us close towards the shoreline. I gripped hold of him by his swim trunks to be sure that I would not lose him on impact, for at that moment I decided that I was going to let the swells take us. The next big swell swept us both towards the bank where Mickey

Caines, the other Elbow Beach lifeguard was standing. Mickey would have been by my side that day had it not been for the managers meeting he was attending. He quickly stepped off the bank into the water and took the boy from me.

As I released the boy, a wave swept in and took me back out to sea. Everyone was so concerned about the boy that they did not realize that I was completely exhausted and could only go with the waves. It was a miracle that I missed hitting the rocks that were being uncovered by the crashing waves. Then a second big wave washed me ashore again, and I tried to dig my hand into the sand to hold on, but I did not have the energy, and I was washed out to sea again, missing the semi-buried boulders. The third time I was washed against the shoreline, a female tourist grabbed me by the arm, but she was not strong enough to pull me ashore. She began screaming for help and two men responded by jumping into the water to assist the woman in pulling me ashore.

When I was pulled ashore, I laid on the bank completely exhausted and cramped. The boy was resuscitated by the ambulance crew and was rushed to the hospital. I never got any of the boys' names, nor did I ever get to meet their families. The reporter who came to the scene that day interviewed several people about what happened, but he never interviewed me. He ended up interviewing my buddy, Mickey who was the one who took the boy from me once I neared the shore.

After about two and a half weeks of the boy being in the hospital, he recovered and was released from the hospital. The family came to Elbow Beach to thank the person who rescued him. The family thanked Mickey, as his name was in the papers, and who relayed their thankfulness to me, but they were never sent down to the beach to speak to me directly. As a result, I never got to see how this survivor was doing. I would have loved to have met them and told them the whole story of the rescue and what their son had gone through.

Southlands Beach

CHAPTER TWENTY-SIX
Celebrity Guests

During my time at Elbow Beach, I had the opportunity to provide hospitality service to many wonderful guests, including many celebrities. Through the Premiere at the time, The Honorable Dr. Ewart Brown, I was able to shake hands with the then current United States President, Mr. Bill Clinton & Mrs. Hilary Clinton on their visit to the Island. These are some of the other celebrities I have had the pleasure of meeting:

> Brooke Shields, Tony Curtis, Janet Leigh, Clint Eastwood, Pat Riley, Red Skelton, Red Fox, Gary Moore, Carol Burnette, Michael Landon, Stevie Wonder, Jack Benny, Alfred Hitchcock, George Hamilton IV, Phil Donahue & Marlo Thomas, Ruby and the Romantics, Chuck Jackson, The Temptations, Ben E. King, The Contours, Mahalia Jackson, Jackie Wilson, The Three Degrees, Cilla Black, Chuck Mangione, Frankie Lymon, Michael & Kirk Douglas, Errol Flynn.

There are many others that I cannot recall at this time.

During the year 1958, a man from abroad made his reservation at Elbow Beach Club, and paid for his hotel stay in full. When this man and woman arrived at the hotel by taxi, it turned out he was a Black man. The bellman went out to retrieve their bags, but really did not know what to do with them, as Blacks were not permitted to stay in the hotel, but he took their bags into the hotel lobby anyway. The Bellman wondered what was going to happen when they checked in, given the segregation policy as many visitors had been turned away before. At this time in Bermuda, Black, Jewish, and other non-White people were not allowed to stay in the hotels. They were being discriminated against. There were several hotels and guest houses owned by Black Bermudians, where many of these guests were permitted to stay.

When the Black man approached the front desk to check in, I happened to be in the Lobby at the time and witnessed this event. He mentioned his name, and explained he paid for a room on the fourth floor overlooking the ocean, and wanted to check in. The receptionist was puzzled, and tried to tell him that there had been some mistake with his booking. She told him he should look into another hotel for his stay. At that time in Bermuda, the Imperial hotel in Hamilton was where Blacks and non-Whites were allowed to stay. This man seemed confused as he paid for his stay at this hotel, and was not backing down. He pulled out his Reservation Confirmation and he stood his ground, as he had paid for his lodging before arrival. The receptionist brought out about five managers or more trying to get this Black man out of there.

All the while, a guest was standing there, watching this situation and how the hotel was handling it. After a few minutes, this guest shouted over "Give that man his room, he has all his documents in order and everything, just give that man his room." This guest who was advocating for the Black man was George Hamilton. The managers decided to compromise by allowing the man to stay at the hotel, but instead of a fourth floor ocean view room, he was given a ground floor room. He was also not allowed in the dining room, and had to receive his meals by room service only. The next year, in 1959, the hotel's policy on segregation was lifted, and the hotels opened up all over the island for everyone to be allowed to stay.

CHAPTER TWENTY-SEVEN
My Three Best Friends

Three of my best friends worked in the hotel industry with me, Maurice Caines, Eardley Jones and Raymond Todd. My friend Maurice "Mikey" Caines, was a very good all-round sportsman. He played cricket, tennis, golf, a very good player of football, and coached for the Hotel International Team. Mickey was responsible for teaching myself and other Bermudians in all of the areas in Hotel Hospitality Services, which helped give Bermuda this glorious reputation of our friendliness and service for our tourism. Raymond Todd, nicknamed "Castro," was one of my best friends. He was a well-known sportsman, outstanding in playing cricket, football, boxing, swimming and loved to run marathons. Another one of my best friends, Eardley Jones, was a good sprinter, played football, cricket, a good billiard player, and an excellent golfer. During his early years of playing golf, Bermuda was still segregated, so the Black Bermudians would have to go on the golf course from five-thirty a.m. to seven a.m., leaving them a very small window to play just a few holes.

Although Eardley was an excellent golfer, he was not allowed to play in any tournaments because the tournaments were played only by Whites and Portuguese men. Eardley had a White American friend, who he caddied for, for many years, and whenever he visited Bermuda to play golf, this friend wanted to play with Eardley. He knew Eardley was good, so he registered him in an upcoming tournament. Eardley won that tournament, causing a great upset for the Bermudian Whites and Portuguese players. As a result of this win, Eardley was not allowed to play in any more tournaments until Bermuda changed its policies allowing Blacks to play in tournaments around 1959. You see, Oceanview Golf course was the only course Blacks could play on at the time. The then Governor, Lord Martonmere went to the management of the prestigious MidOcean Golf Club and the Ocean View Golf Club to make arrangements for a tournament called the "Martonmere Cup" - that opened the doors for all Bermudians golfers to be able to play.

As I mentioned, all three of my best friends worked in the hotel industry and were all well-known for their outstanding customer service going the extra mile for our Island visitors. In the early 80's, Bermuda experienced some of its roughest water that were effects coming from the different storms or hurricanes that were passing between Bermuda and the U.S. coastline. On this particular day "Castro" went to Horseshoe Bay to run, knowing he could not swim that day because of the roughness of the water. While running eastward toward Warwick Long Bay, Castro suddenly heard a lady screaming and crying, *"John, come back, John come back!"* Raymond, without saying a word to the woman, saw that this John fellow was in trouble and caught in an undertow, so he immediately threw off his shoes and swam out to John to help him out of the undertow.

Once Raymond helped John out of the under tow, John made his own way into shore and lay there from exhaustion, which is when his wife realized that the man who helped her husband, Castro (though she did not know his name), was in trouble. She was very aware that she nor her husband were not in a condition to help him, and she ran all the way to the top of the hill to South Shore Road screaming and waving out to all the traffic for someone to come and help. There was so much traffic backed up along the road and all the way down to the beach, but with all the people there, no one wanted to go into the water, as it was quite turbulent. When the policemen arrived on the scene, they too did not want to go into the water, and they decided that they would send a squad car to the Elbow Beach Hotel, because they knew that Elbow Beach had two of the best lifeguards on the Island, Mickey Canes and myself.

When the police arrived at the hotel beach, Mickey first asked me to go, and just as I was getting in the car, he decided that he would go himself. While Eardley Jones was out on his postal route, he passed by Warwick Long Bay, and saw all the traffic and commotion, and decided to ride down to the Beach to see what it was all about. He could see that someone was in trouble and immediately took off his shirt and shoes, passed his wallet to one of the policemen as he prepared to go in. Eardley took a life-ring, with a long rope attached to it from the police officer, but upon entering the water had great difficulty just getting past the large waves. He managed to throw the life-ring over a large wave coming up and simultaneously dove under that wave. When he re-surfaced the life-ring was there for him.

Eardley had to swim quite a distance out to the person in trouble, and when he finally reached the person, he realized that it was his friend Castro! When Eardley finally was able to put the life-ring around Castro, Castro started to relax as he had been struggling in the sea water for nearly two hours. By now Castro and Eardley had drifted westward behind a large rock, and at this time the policemen were pulling on the rope attached to the life-ring. The policemen did not realize that they were pulling Castro and Eardley into more danger towards the rocks and the reefs, and when Eardley tried to signal to them by waving and shouting at them to stop pulling, the policemen could not hear him as the sounds of the rough waves crashing against the rocks were drowning his voice out, misread his signaling, and the policemen kept pulling.

Mickey arrived in the police car just in time to stop the policemen from further pulling Castro and Eardley toward more danger into the rocks and the reefs, as he shouted "*Stop, Stop, let the rope go!*". At this point he took the rope and jogged eastward about one hundred feet where he could see Castro and Eardley clearly, and was able to help them maneuver clear of the rocks. When Mickey could see that they were clear of the dangerous rocks and reefs, he was able to pull them in safety. Everyone was exhausted, but the woman was very thankful to Castro for saving her husband John. Castro was very thankful to his friend Eardley for coming to his rescue, and both Castro and Eardley were very thankful to their friend Mickey who came back to the beach to let me know what actually happened. It was a good thing Castro was running on the beach in the first place. Eardley was a postman for many years, and eventually retired and became a professional golfer. He also loved to teach the sport of golf to the youth of Bermuda.

Me playing golf

CHAPTER TWENTY-EIGHT
You Are Officially in The Race

While working at Elbow Beach Carpenter Shop in the early 60's, there was an English gentleman by the name of Jock Shanks who was teaching me the trade of carpentry. Quite often he would share stories with me whenever he went to watch the runners competing at the Bermuda Athletic Association (BAA) field by running laps around the field and he would often tell me how the foreign boys, who were Englishman working and living in Bermuda would leave the Bermudian boys behind by 3 or 4 laps. I would say to him, "*I would never let anyone leave me behind by that many laps!*"

Shortly after making that statement, there was an announcement made by BAA to all the Sports Clubs that they were looking for footballers to compete in Running Competitions at the BAA Field. After the announcement, Lee Tucker, the Team Manager of the Bombardiers for The Warwick Workman's Club, picked six of us to run at the BAA Field, and we all accepted. I had heard and read about some of the Team members who participated in these Competitions at the BAA field, such as those from the Police Department; who were the likes of Jeff Payne, Tony Harper, Mensies, Cricklow, and the well-known runners from BAA who were, Boarman and David Saul, and also those from The Social Club, who were David Landy and Kid Tucker.

The selected team chosen by Lee Tucker was really excited to go and compete up against these well-known runners. The American Navy and the Air-Force Bases, together with The Canadian Base who were occupied in Bermuda at that time, also sent their selected runners to compete in this Competition. The two American runners selected for the Competition were also hopefuls for the Americans for the U.S. Olympic Games, but in the Competition, they could not beat David Landy, who was Bermuda's fastest 100-yard Dash runner and capable of winning a medal for Bermuda, if he was given a chance to enter the Olympics. Once the excitement of being selected wore off, my thoughts went to the fact that I had never practiced for a competition or run a mile, which was 8 laps around the field, but I was still excited to go to BAA to compete and my main motivation was to show Mr. Shanks that nobody would leave me three or four laps behind!

    The evening of the Competition when it was my time to run and I heard the announcer say, "*When the gun goes off, the race will start,*" and he then sarcastically said "*When you hear the bell ring that will mean you have one lap to go and I know that most of you would not be there.*" When the race took off, Jeff Payne intentionally lagged behind to hold back the rest of the field runners, because he knew he could catch up and beat the ones in front of him. While holding the field back, I touched him on his heel, and he took off like a Jack Rabbit straight to the front, and I continued to stay with him. After doing three laps, I am thinking to myself "*How can I stay up with them for the next five laps?*" but surprisingly, I stayed with him, not knowing where this energy was coming from. Starting on the 6th lap, I could hear the crowd saying, "*Who is that little fellow?*" and I just kept running and then I heard that bell ring. Knowing this was the last lap, I realized that the front runners started to speed up and somehow my determination allowed me to keep up with them, right to the Finish Line and I ended up coming in third.

After the race, I flopped onto the ground totally exhausted with my chest burning as if it were on fire, when Jock Shanks came up to me and with excitement, said, "*Man, I am really proud of you. You can run, you really surprised me because you've never trained for this type of race, because you are a football player, so just imagine if you had trained for this race!*" After the race finished, Lee Tucker, the Team Manager, recognized that I had set a new record as the fastest Junior Runner at the BAA for the One Mile Race and when he approached the officials so that they could announce this, they were a bit hesitant, because based on my performance they were not sure that I was a junior, and also because earlier they had announced that their junior team member, who I had left behind by three laps, held the previous record.

The next day after the competition, Jock Shanks came to me like a proud father, and he was all around the hotel bragging about how fast I could run, and how I had set a new Junior record at the BAA Track and Field Competition, without any training for the One Mile Race. After competing in my first One Mile Race and setting a new record at the BAA Competitions, I continued to play football, but my interest kept going to the idea of running track. Shortly after seeing my performance, two of my friends, Forthy Rego and Eddie Simons kept encouraging me to run track. After the competition at BAA they told me that there was a 10K race being held at the Botanical Gardens around ten a.m. that day and that I should try to enter. I jumped on my bike and raced to the Botanical Gardens and arrived ten minutes before the race started. The one thing that I noticed when I got there was that I was the only Black person entering the race, and when I asked the officials if I could enter, they welcomed me and said "*Yes, you can enter.*"

Just before the start of the race, I realized that I had my track pants on, stepped back and sat down on the ground behind the starting line. When the official said to me "*Hurry up, the race is about to start,*" before I could get my pants off, the race had started. I then realized that I could not take my track pants off before taking off my shoes and by the time I had taken the shoes off, and then the track pants, and then put the shoes back on, by this time all the runners had a three-minute lead on me. The official said to me, "*You have a lot of catching up to do, but you are officially in the race!*"

When I caught up with the slower runners, they were as far as Demo Flower shop, which is a half of a mile from the Botanical Gardens. At Devonshire Bay, I caught up with the leaders, one of whom was David Saul, a well-known sportsman, but unfortunately, I could not pass them, only because I did not know the route of the race. So I paced myself by running behind them, and because they did not run as fast as I could, I was becoming very frustrated, and burning up unnecessary energy. When we reached Tuckers Town there was a crowd of people who knew David Saul, and they were all calling out to him and he answered back to them by calling a few names.

When we reached the turning point and after running about one hundred yards, I realized that we were going back on the same route, and this was my opportunity to finally break away from the pack. When I reached John Smith's Bay, I glanced back and did not see a soul in sight, so I just kept trucking along. By the time I reached The Harrington Sound grocery store, which was one of the longest stretches, I looked behind me and once again I did not see a soul in sight, and for a minute I wondered to myself, "*Am I going the right way, or did I make a wrong turn?*" Several times while running down McGall's Hill and onto The Apothecary, I kept glancing back but still did not see anyone in sight, but I kept going on that route until I reached the final stretch at Tee Street. At Tee Street, I sped up until I reached about fifty yards before the finish line, and to my surprise there were five or six people who locked arms together to form a human chain blocking me from crossing the finish line, and told me that I could not go to the finish line. They guided me off to the side of the road, and I went behind the finish line, put on my track suit and sat on my bike. It was a good twelve minutes before Dr. David Saul came into sight and had at least three minutes to get to the Finish Line where they announced him as 'The Winner' and that he had set a record. After seeing what happened I started my bike and left.

    Years later, whenever I attended meetings on any political issues that were going on in Bermuda, Dr. David Saul, who, by that time had become the Premier of Bermuda, was always there and quite often acted as a spokesman. Somehow, he always bragged about a race that he ran from The Botanical Gardens to Tucker's Town and back, and how he set a record and how it had never been broken. For the longest time whenever I heard him brag, I wanted to approach him to speak with him about that race, but I was not given the opportunity for one reason or the other to do so, and no one ever came forward to address what had happened to me at the finish line. I wanted to tell him that I believe that the time they gave him for setting that record was my time!

Many years later while listening to Mark 'Burger' Jennings, the host on the most popular Radio Sport Talk Show in Bermuda which airs three nights a week and talks about local sports, World Sports and includes sports from A-Z and is very informative. It is also very exciting to hear stories from our local sportsmen, men and women, plus the general public about their experiences in sport events taking place in Bermuda, and it was on this show that I heard Mark talk about how Dr. David Saul had run a race from the Botanical Gardens to Tucker's Town and back and had set a record and that record had never been broken! Well, I thought to myself that this was my opportunity to set the record straight, so I called into the talk show and finally got to tell my side of the story. The next time I called the talk show, I called Mark to ask him if he had mentioned my side of the story to Dr. David Saul and he said that when he did, David told him that he had heard something, but he said *"Something happened, but I did NOT know what!"* The fact that I was finally able to tell my side of the story to the general public gives me great satisfaction to this day.

CHAPTER TWENTY-NINE
Going to The Record Hops

My dating years were some of the roughest years of my young life. When I was between the ages of sixteen and eighteen and was becoming interested in girls, they were starting to show interest in me. I was a fit person, was considered a gentleman, and would take flowers when I picked up a girl. I was a conservative dresser, and the neighbors all called me the gentlemen. They all could trust me with their daughters, the parents would let them go out with me. After a while, the young ladies seemed to start to pull away from me, eventually losing interest. I found out it was because my friends would always get to them and tell them that they should not become my friend because I was too black, had kinky knotty hair, and that I came from the "Poor House." After being teased by my friends, the girls would always back off. I finally got to a point where I did not even want to talk to a light-skinned pretty girl, who had what was considered "good hair." because of my lack of confidence. It seemed that every guy liked the soft haired, light-skinned pretty girls, and my Grandfather even told me, "*If you want to be happy for the rest of your life, never marry a pretty woman for your wife.*"

I was feeling left out of the scene. One of the other things that made me feel left out, was the fact that I did not drink, cuss or smoke, and was always polite and well dressed. Most of the girls seemed to look at these things as being a "square" and not cool. A square was a term that was used to describe someone who folks considered straightforward, acceptable, safe. I always felt that I was not a part of the group and felt left out in the cold.

During this time, when I did get dates, many times the girls used me as their date to get out of their house. They knew if I asked their parents if I could take them to the Record Hops, the parents would say yes, because their parents trusted me, had always referred to me as a gentleman, and knew that I would get their daughters back home on time. But once we got to the dances, I would never see those girls again until it was time to take them back home, and they would be off dancing with other guys.

Over time all the teasing, insults, name calling, and consistently being embarrassed by my friends, this made me very shy to the point of not trusting women, because they always ran off with other guys. Whenever I did manage to get a dance with another girl, guys would come and interrupt us and the girls would go off with them. This ritual of escorting these young girls to the Record Hops went on until I reached the age of eighteen and started to go to nightclubs to see my sister Violeta perform. My sister Violeta was a phenomenal singer with a band, and during this time I started to meet other women who were visiting the island. In most cases these women would be older than myself and they appreciated me for who I was and not because of the color of my skin, or my kinky knotty hair or the fact that I came from the Poor House.

When I started to go to the nightclubs instead of the Record Hops and my friends would see me out with foreign women, they would say to me, "*Hey Rene, I only see you with the Pink Ladies and the Long tails, what happened to the sparrows?*" What they meant by that is the local Bermudian girls were referred to as Sparrows; which are local birds to the Island. The Black foreign women were referred to as Long Tails, because they, like the birds, return to Bermuda in the summers, and the White women were referred to as Pink Ladies. After a while I found it ironic that the same friends who teased me and caused the local girls not to be interested in me, now wanted _me_ to show them how they could be set up with these mature foreign women! Ironically, after eleven years of only going out with foreign women, my first date with a Bermudian woman, ended up becoming my wife, but that is a story for another chapter.

A young Renalda

CHAPTER THIRTY
It's All in Divine Order

In 1956 at the age of thirteen while working at the Elbow Beach Hotel, one day while standing in line in the staff dining room for lunch, there was a woman by the name of Adora Smith who was either always standing in front of me or immediately behind me. This particular day, Mrs. Smith was behind me and being the gentleman that I am, I offered for her to go in front of me and she responded by saying, "*No, no, you don't little fellow, you see all those women behind you, you would never get any lunch.*" What she meant is that I would probably let many of the women go in front of me to get their food being polite, and I would be left with none. After getting to know Mrs. Smith, she recognized the good qualities that I had, and she said to me "*I have a nice little girl home for you,*" but at that time, at the age of thirteen I was not even interested in girls.

In 1969, while watching Chuck Jackson from New York perform at the Forty Thieves Club, I noticed a group of about ten local girls sitting near the front of the dance floor. During the interval, the music would start and everybody would get up and dance, and when I checked out the table where the local girls were sitting, I now noticed that there was only one girl sitting there alone. She was a beautiful young lady, and I went over and put my hand out to dance, and she accepted. We danced two dances and she then went back to her seat, and I never saw her again.

A few months later, I went to a friend's wedding, and lo and behold, she was one of the bride's maids. I just saw her there, did not speak or anything. Shortly after my friend's wedding, I was working as a beach attendant at Elbow Beach Club, and my friend approached me to ask if his wife and her co-workers could come and spend a few hours at the beach. He explained to me that his wife and her co-workers were nurses and they worked twelve-hour shifts, and they wanted to swim and sunbathe so they could go back home and sleep until their next shift. I agreed to let them come and spend a few hours.

On the nurses first visit to the beach, I recognized one of the young ladies as the one who I had danced with at the Forty Thieves Club a few months earlier. Knowing I had not been out with local women for many years, I thought I would ask this young lady if she would like to go with me to the Hamilton Princess to see "The Three Degrees", a female singing group from America, who were at the top of the Rock and Roll music chart. She responded by saying "*No,*" and I stood there and watched her walk back on the beach to her friends.

Within the next three minutes after the rejection of the beautiful young lady, along came a pretty young blonde guest of the hotel, who was alone and had just arrived from Boston. She asked me about the entertainment around the island, and I told her about the Three Degrees at the Princess. She then asked me about her being alone going to a nightclub, and then I said "*If you want to go, I would be happy to take you,*" and with excitement she responded " *Yes!*" and gave me her room number to call when I was ready to pick her up. Shortly after she left, the young lady who had rejected me earlier came back and asked me if the date was still open. Now, in my excitement, I said " *Yes*" and at that point she introduced herself as Ela. I then realized that I had to go and call the other young lady who had just accepted my invitation and lie to her by telling her that I had to work late.

Ela and I had agreed to meet at the Hamilton Princess, and when I walked up, I saw her standing outside of the nightclub and to my surprise, there were nine other people there with her, a mix of guys and other girls. We all went in, and at the end of a very good show all of the guys left the table to go into the Men's room to settle the bill, which was a customary thing to do at the time. While in there settling the bill, three of the guys left the men's room and the only two that were left were myself and my buddy. My buddy then said to me "L*ooks like they don't have any money*," and we said to one another "*I guess we have to pay.*" So, we ended up splitting the bill.

When we left the hotel, we then went to a restaurant called Greens which was located on Court Street, which was not far from Ela's home on Angle Street. From the restaurant I gave her a ride on my bike to the entrance of her home and she jumped off the bike, kissed me on the cheek and ran up the stairs. As I rode home, I thought to myself, "*I don't think I would be going out with her again, because I felt I was used.*" I felt I was being used because during the whole evening I never had a chance to get to know her just because of all the other people who were invited and I felt it was just supposed to be the two of us. The whole experience of this reminded me of how my interactions used to be when I was younger taking the girls to the Record Hops, and how they would go off with other guys.

Three weeks after taking Ela out, I was invited to a friend's house who was having his twin boys christened. When I entered the living room there were many women there, and to my surprise, I saw Ela. Being the only man as I looked upon the room, I immediately said *"Good evening one and all"* and made a quick turn to get out of that room. Once I got outside, there were all of the Bombardiers players from Warwick Workman's Club who I played football with, and I joined them in their conversation. An hour and a half after my arrival, Ela came out and stood near me and I just continued talking with my buddies trying to ignore her. My friends had realized that Ela was trying to talk with me so they were inching slowly away from me, but I kept making conversation in my effort to keep them there, trying my best to avoid Ela. After at least twenty minutes of my avoiding her, Ela interrupted and said to me, *"Good Evening Mr. Bean, you're not speaking,"* and I replied, *"when I arrived I said good evening one and all,"* and then I said to her, *"Would you wait a minute"* and she did, so I bid my farewells to my friends by telling them that I would talk with them later.

When we finally got the opportunity to talk, I said to her, *"For the past three weeks, I have heard from many of your friends how you had a great time at the show at the Princess,"* and I then said to her *"You didn't give me the chance to say anything to you, to get to know you, you just kiss me on the cheek and ran off."* I then said to her, *"I felt that I had been used, because I had invited you, but there were nine other people, and I'm letting you know that if you think I want you for sex, you can forget it."* At this point she started to cry, and I then said to her *"Who's taking you home?"* She said that her girlfriends were. I then told her to tell her friends that I would take her, and we could stop at the Parquet Restaurant for tea or coffee. We ended up stopping at the restaurant, having some tea and finally getting to know one another. When we arrived at her house, I told her that "*I am not serious about being in a relationship,*" and she said the same, but we then both agreed that we would go out occasionally.

Ela and I had been out on a number of dates, and it was nearing the time that I would normally be taking vacation, so when I told her that I was going away for five or six weeks, she said that "*I was stopping someone from living their life.*" I completely ignored her words and I left for New York shortly afterward. After two weeks of being in New York, I had time to think about the words that she had said to me about stopping someone from living their life, and this made me think to myself, "*Some of my friends are married and most of them have children who were teenagers and at the age of twenty-eight, and I have none.*" This was something I wanted in my life, and after having that thought, I picked up the phone and called her, and when she answered, I knew her voice immediately. I then said to her "*Would you have children for me?*" and her response was "*If we get married,*" and I said, "*Okay, I will see when I get back.*" When I left Bermuda to go to New York, I had taken seven bottles of "Chanel No. Five" perfume to give to my lady friends in New York, but when I returned to Bermuda, I ended up bringing back five of the seven bottles, which I gave to my sisters, because I did not want to give Ela a bottle which I had brought for other women.

After Ela and I had been going out on several more dates, one Saturday night she asked me if she could spend the night at my place. I agreed and I surprised myself because I never allowed anyone to spend the night. The next morning, when I left for work Ela was still sleeping and when I returned home later, she had cleaned my house, cooked a big dinner and to my surprise, she had a large towel spread across my kitchen table with a lot of money on it! She told me that as she was cleaning, every time she came across a lump in the carpet, she found money, lots of money. After finding all of this money just laying around, Ela said to me "*You need to open a bank account, and if you have any more money anywhere else, you should put it all in the bank.*" Having made this suggestion, I knew I had ten thousand dollars in the ceiling rolled up with a rubber band, so I pushed up the wooden plank and when I reached in to take the money down, and to my surprise, it was just crumbled paper, as the rats had chewed it to smithereens! A few days later I put all the money that had accumulated into my first bank account, minus the ten thousand dollars that the rats had chewed up!

The following week after staying overnight at my apartment, Ela asked me if I would come and meet her mother. Shortly after that, when I went to pick Ela up to go on a date, she invited me in and introduced me to her mother. Well, I was totally shocked and could not believe my eyes, because it was Mrs. Adora Smith, the same woman who told me in 1957, when I was only fourteen, that she had a nice little girl home for me, which was some thirteen years earlier!

In February of 1971, I celebrated my twenty-eighth birthday by having a party at my apartment and had invited many of my friends and Ela had invited a few of hers. Secretly, I had brought Ela an engagement ring to present to her on my birthday. The surprise of it all was the fact that I had purchased a tray of gold wrapped chocolate coins and had asked my sister if she would ask Ela to pass them out to the guests. As she was passing them out, the guests noticed the engagement ring taped to the center chocolate coin on the top layer of the chocolates, but Ela never noticed it and her friends were following her like a train all around the house as she was handing them out, trying to give her hints. Finally, they all surrounded her and said "*Ela, look at the tray of chocolates!*" When Ela finally saw the ring, her knees buckled and she broke down and cried and gave me a big hug and kiss.

On October twenty first 1973, Ela and I married. Out of this union, my daughter, Angela Renee was born August 8, 1974, and my son, Renalda Judiah Bermudaz, was born July 15th, 1977. In 1977, when my son was two months old, my sister Verlice called me to ask if I had seen the picture that was taken in 1964, of my football team boarding a plane when we were visiting New York, Montreal and Toronto. I told her "*Yes, I had it in my album.*" She then asked if I had seen the picture on the opposite side and when I looked at the picture, to my surprise, it was my wife Ela, who I did not know at the time and four other girls who were going off to England to study nursing, because I met Ela in 1969, five years after the picture was taken. All I can say is that everything happens in divine order!

CHAPTER THIRTY-ONE

Second Act

After my 1997 retirement, in 1998 I took on driving taxi. My goal in purchasing a taxi was to continue in hospitality, but also improve the service of taxi operations across the island. It seemed that many of the taxi drivers were driving their tourist customers from point A to point B, but the "Bermudian Hospitality" that we were famous for on our little island was missing. Our tourists were not getting a true Bermudian welcoming experience. Before I started driving the taxi, all I knew about my island was to and from work, even traveling to the city of Hamilton and back. There were of course Special Events such as County Games throughout the Island, and Cup Match, which is held in Somerset or St. Georges, but I was even unaware of the many various beautiful places of the Island myself.

The minute I started to drive taxi, I was seeing a different Bermuda, as I was taking people to their private homes all across the whole island. These were places and houses you would never think were there until you got there. One night, I picked up a pair of tourists from a restaurant around nine-thirty p.m. From the moment they entered the car, I welcomed them, and started to ask questions like how were they enjoying their stay on the island, and how long had they been here. They explained this was their last night in Bermuda, and I began explaining things to them about Bermuda, talking about the beaches and scenery while I was driving to their hotel. When I got to the hotel, the guests were very pleased and commented, although it is dark, we were still able to see the beauty of this island as I was explaining it. They mentioned that when they arrived, they got in a taxi at the airport, and the driver never said anything to them during the entire ride to the hotel. They said, " *We would love for you to come pick us up tomorrow morning at six a.m. to go to the airport.*"

I agreed, and the next day when I arrived at the hotel, hotel security had three other taxi's lined up for their guests. I tell him I am here to pick up two guests, I describe them, and he tells me they are gone. I was puzzled wondering why they would tell me to pick them up early and then leave, but I decided to wait a minute and within two minutes the guy comes out and says he will be ready in another ten minutes. He was so pleased to see me, and I took them to the airport while giving them a tour of the island, and got them there within plenty of time.

Several taxi drivers at one time approached me because as I did my job driving taxi, I used to give tourists explanations of the sights around Bermuda as we were going along to their destinations. The other drivers wanted me to stop explaining so much, because "they are not going to take a tour after that". I told them, "*Let me tell you all, I'm NOT going to stop it because you do what you all want to do, and my goal is to give the best service to my customers. By doing so, it entices them to take tours and see more of our wonderful island.*" In the years since I have retired from Elbow Beach, I have been able to drive my taxi for twenty-three years, and even received a special certificate for service in hospitality for wheelchair accessibility of my taxi. The taxi service is one of the highs in my life now as I get to show off beautiful Bermuda as I show them everything they can possibly see, feel and smell of Bermuda. I want to make sure that their experience is as pleasant as it can be, if it is within my authority to make it. I typically end my tours with some poetry or words that I authored that captures my love of Bermuda:

Taxi

© 1998 Renalda Bean
I am of solid rock and limestone
I am of coral reef and pink sand
I am of crystal blue waters much like the sky
I am of beautiful blossomed flowers and their perfume
I am one of many who welcomes you, my friends!
When you gaze upon the beauty I am sharing with you...
I am of one man's island
I am a Bermudian Taxi Driver!

CONCLUSION

In my many years and my numerous adventures- as a boy, a son, a brother, a teen, a lifeguard, husband, a father, a Black Man, etc.; I have learned countless lessons along the way about people. I began writing these stories for my children, who may have not known about how hard life was in Bermuda before their time. There were a myriad of obstacles and triumphs throughout my life for some of the things that have happened. For other things that have happened, there were no real explanations or repercussions, and I was just expected to deal with the way the world was. It was not often that we were able to speak our truths back then, or even now, but it is important to do so.

As a person who was not expected to achieve much, being from what was considered the poor house, to people putting me down in various ways, ending my formal education early on, I was determined to make a pathway for my family and build a legacy. I hope these stories help educate people about some of the history and the beauty and the pride and love I have for Bermuda, through my eyes and my heart which means one love for all.

ADDENDUM

◆

Key Points You Should Know About the Portuguese Man-Of-War

I, Willard Renalda Bean, nicknamed "Rene" would like to share my knowledge and key points about the Portuguese-Man-of-War. In my many years as a lifeguard I had been stung at least a hundred times all over my body, which included my eyes, nose, lips, mouth, ears, armpits, right down to my toes and even the inside of my bathing trunks. Having been stung so many times, I have taught myself a number of techniques on how to pick a Portuguese-Man-of-War out of the water without getting stung, and also how to remove the tentacles one by one from off the body, by using a towel without causing more damage. I also taught myself how to apply holistic treatment, by using vinegar, ammonia and olive oil which neutralize the acid, but does not stop the pain.

Please note, I am not a medical professional, and you should immediately seek medical attention as needed if your circumstances warrant.

- The Portuguese man of war is not a friend to mankind. It would give you severe pains that would last all of four hours, depending on how one's body reacts.
- The Portuguese man of war tentacles could leave scarring on your body for a week or in some cases a whole year or more.
- The Portuguese-Man-of-War can extend its many tentacles from two inches to forty feet or more.
- The Portuguese-Man-of-War cannot extend its tentacles at you because the tentacles are behind them, so always swim in front of them, and the reason for this is, it's movement goes with the current or the wind, depending on which one is stronger at the time.
- The Portuguese-Man-of-War's only movement is when it trips itself in the water to wet its upper body.

- When stung by the Portuguese-Man-of-War, the pain is extremely excruciating. It feels like several bees have stung you at the same time.
- If you are ever stung by The Portuguese-Man-of-War on the hand, which is one of the most sensitive parts of your body, your hand is most likely to swell. After three hours of being stung anywhere on your hand or arm, you will later feel a numbness from your armpit to your collarbone nerve center. This is indicating that within the next hour, the pain will subside, but the scarring may stay for a while.
- If you get stung on your leg or foot, the numbness starts from the inner side of your knee to your crotch, and this would be a sign that within the hour the pain will completely stop.

I have tried many techniques to find a remedy to stop the pain of a Portuguese Man-of-War sting, but have never found anything to be successful, and I have never known anyone to be sick beyond the pain described. For many years there was a belief that urinating on a person would help to take away the pain. That is not true, it is a lie. In my many experiences of dealing with the Portuguese-Man-of-War, I have learned there are certain things that you "Do and not Do:"

- Never try to pick up a Portuguese-Man-of-War out of the water
- Never poke a Portuguese-Man-of-War with a stick, because someone can touch the stick later and get stung, because the tentacles stay alive for a while which is until they completely dry up.
- Never pop a Portuguese-Man-of-War with a stick, because this can cause toxic gases to be released and it could be dangerous and may affect the eyes.
- Never let anyone rub sand on a Man-of-War sting, as this can cause more damage and irritation to the skin

- Never use anything to try to rub the tentacles off, as this causes more pain, because each tentacle MUST be pulled off individually, preferable with a towel.
- Never panic if you have been stung! Tell yourself that this is going to be painful, and try to get the tentacles off immediately with some assistance (depending on the placement of the Man of War) or by yourself, remembering to remove tentacles one by one.
- Never forget that the pain is going to be with you for at least four hours.
- Try not to panic when you feel the numbness in any part of your body, as this is a sign that the pain will completely stop within the next hour.
- Never urinate on Portuguese-Man-of-War sting, because it's nasty and it does not help.

ABOUT THE AUTHOR

Willard Renalda Bean is a man of many talents. Born and raised in Bermuda in 1943, he has endured and thrived in many ways on this wonderful island with GOD and his family by his side. Throughout his years, he challenged himself to always do better and to try and make a difference to any persons he encountered.

Among the talents outlined in this book, he was a dedicated runner, an avid traveler (pre-pandemic) and lover of fishing and golf. In his spare time, he enjoyed making kites and is currently very passionate about gardening at his homestead and the community garden. With the support of his family, his loving wife of 48 years Ela, his children and grandchildren, "Rene" was encouraged to document his stories for all to hear.

This book shares just some of his adventures.

ABOUT THE AMANUENSIS

These stories were told to Ms. Pamela Ramsay. Pamela Jean Ramsay was born and raised on the beautiful Island of Bermuda. She is passionate about discovering the true meaning of life and is equally passionate to share with others her knowledge, wisdom, and spirituality that she has gained throughout her life's journey. Pamela is an avid reader. This love for reading has readily complemented her skill in helping to type and edit manuscripts. While working on this manuscript and to help the author bring his stories to life, she was able to share his journey; in a sense "re-living" his experiences with him. This process was deeply gratifying and a true honor for her.

Pamela's other interests includes cooking, spending time with family and friends and enjoying nature; which includes feeding a flock of wild birds that gather in her backyard daily. It is her hope that the enjoyment that she experienced while working with the author, will also bring enjoyment to his readers.

ABOUT THE EDITOR

Natasha E. Bean is the daughter of Melvin S. Bean, Renalda's second brother. She was born in the Bronx, New York, USA and consistently travels to Bermuda to visit her many family members. She is a lifelong learner, poet, author, and avid lover of all things creative- whether it is painting, making jewelry or pursuing her photography. When her Uncle mentioned he was working on a book, immediately she was intrigued as learning about the history of Bermuda coupled with the geology of their family seemed fascinating and amazing. Throughout this process, there were many discoveries about how idyllic Bermuda is juxtaposing against Black Bermudian resident's experiences and how Bermuda treated its visitors overall. Working with him to complete these stories has truly opened her eyes.

Natasha is a graduate of Manhattan College, NY with a B.S. in Business Administration & Management and a Masters of Arts degree in Higher Education & Student Affairs from New York University where she is the Director of Financial Education.

www.ingramcontent.com/pod-product-compliance
Lightning Source LLC
Chambersburg PA
CBHW072156160426
43197CB00012B/2407